Abuse & Betrayal

The Cautionary True Story of Divorce, Mistakes, Lies and Legal Abuse

By
Richard Joseph

Copyright © 2014 Richard Joseph
All rights reserved.
ISBN: 1494845946
ISBN 13: 9781494845940

Contents

Introduction: My Story

PART 1

1. Happy Beginnings 3
2. From Happy to Empty 9
3. Inappropriate Behavior 17
4. Counseling & Divorce 31
5. Lies & Dysfunctional Behavior 41
6. Arrested 57
7. Hurtful Betrayal 73
8. Prison 85
9. Losing the Girls 111
10. Moving Away 121

PART 2

11. Narcissistic Personality Disorder 135
12. Parental Alienation Syndrome 145
13. Divorce Related Malicious Parent Syndrome 155
14. Legal Abuse Syndrome 161
15. National Coalition Against Parental Alienation (NCAPA) 169

Disclosure

This story is entirely true. I have not embellished or fabricated any part of it.

In an effort to protect my daughters I have changed the names of all the parties involved.
This book is published under my partial name for the same reason.

It is not my intent to harass or libel anyone.
I simply want to make this story available to people who may benefit from it.

Richard Joseph

Introduction

When I first got the idea to write this book, I felt a sense of purpose—almost relief—in the thought that I might be able to use my hellish experience to create a context for understanding and healing for myself. I knew I was a long way from truly achieving either, but my energy was lifted and sustained by the hope that I might actually be capable of finding at least some inner peace. It also dawned on me that by articulating the lessons learned from my suffering I might actually help others in similar circumstances to feel less alone, angry, and helpless. I also thought my story might speak to some of the millions of people suffering from a stressful marriage (and who will eventually join the ranks of the divorced), enabling them to avoid the mistakes I made and sparing them at least some of the damage and pain. I have tried to honestly point out these mistakes, as I've tried to articulate my pain and heartbreak.

This is my story. Every bit of it is true, and much of it is sad. Telling this story was cathartic for me in some ways, emotional in many others. It is never easy to admit your mistakes, but the biggest mistake of all is not learning from the ones you've already made.

I'm sure that most people are unfamiliar with terms such as Parental Alienation Syndrome and Legal

Abuse Syndrome. Before my divorce, I certainly was. The idea that a parent would purposely work to alienate children from the other parent through custody violations, lies, and legal harassment is not a possibility I had considered. Not only did I think that no one could be that devious or heartless, but I assumed the legal divorce process was built on fairness, with a series of checks and balances to ensure significant abuse couldn't possibly occur without appropriate recourse and correction.

I also assumed that attorneys in family practice were especially ethical in this incredibly sensitive area of the law, which affects families in such profound ways as where the children will live, how often they will see each parent, and the monetary realities of everyone's immediate future. After all, I thought, divorce wasn't necessarily a situation of parental neglect or abuse, but rather the dissolution of the bonds between adults. And adult parents, I believed, should be able to move on without destroying everything built along the way that was good and useful.

With the recent societal focus on issues surrounding single-parent families, and particularly absentee fathers, I assumed everyone's objective would be to ensure that a man who had dedicated himself to being a good father, someone who had provided a stable financial and emotional foundation for the family, would remain a significant presence in the lives of his kids. Why would anyone, especially a mother, want to deny the benefits of a good father to their kids? Why would a father deserve a less significant role once the original family unit was dissolved?

In short, I assumed everyone involved in the divorce process, including parents, attorneys, and the legal system itself would work to do what was best for the separated family, especially the kids. I wasn't entirely naïve, though. I knew of people who had difficult marital breakups and heartbreaking family circumstances. But to me, those stories represented a small minority of cases—the exceptions—not the average divorce. With approximately half of all marriages ending in divorce, I assumed that the system worked well as a general rule.

I soon found out that, in too many divorces, these assumptions are as naïve as expecting our politicians to work together harmoniously and in the best interests of the country. When the realities of selfishness, hidden agendas, legal machinations, personality disorders, and control issues are introduced into a system that many times is unfairly biased to begin with, the assumption of fairness can be quickly shattered.

This is the story of my own shattered assumptions and the perfect storm of issues and circumstances that shattered my relationship with my girls and left me wondering how, after seventeen years of being a faithful husband and a great father, I could end up being abandoned and abused by those who were the focus of my life for so long.

PART 1

Chapter 1

Happy Beginnings

I met my ex-wife through mutual friends when I was twenty-nine years old. Diane was twenty-three and living in central New Jersey. I was living in southern New Jersey, close to where I had grown up. I had ended a serious relationship about a year earlier and was ready to find someone special. Diane was in the final stages of her first divorce, a warning sign (among others) I ignored at the time.

I was attracted to Diane....tall and slender with auburn hair and green eyes. To her credit (and genetic luck), she doesn't look much different now. Men have always responded to her appearance, and I was no different. One of the problems with being young is the difficulty in differentiating between the feelings of love in a fundamentally important sense and the enjoyment of sex. It was a lesson learned: love typically includes sex, but loving the sex you're having with someone is *not* necessarily love.

By the time we met, I had a bachelor's degree in finance and had already established myself as a self-employed consultant specializing in helping clients in the financial services industry generate additional revenues through strategic partnerships. I was paying my bills, and all indications pointed to a secure future. Diane hadn't gone to college, but instead attended secretarial school. She was doing fairly well as an executive assistant at a biotech company.

I didn't focus at the time on some significant differences between us. For example, I enjoyed reading, learning, and stimulating conversation, but Diane's priorities had always been different. And alcohol wasn't particularly important to me, as it was to her. I also thought it was a bit strange that, while I still had close friends dating back to my high school days, she seemed to be all alone in the world. Given her social skills and extroverted personality, her lack of close friends should have been another red flag. But again, while I was in a position to notice things like this, I wasn't interested in focusing on negatives at that point in my life. I suspect differences like these are routinely overlooked by people with the idea of starting a family on their minds. Diane definitely had street smarts though, and coupled with her good looks, it was enough to keep me interested.

Neither one of us had had a structurally-sound family situation growing up. She had lost her biological father to a congenital heart condition when she was very young. Her mom had been subjected to a very difficult childhood herself, which left her with severe emotional issues. Unfortunately, she has been institutionalized several times. As a result of these circumstances, Diane became more assertive at a younger age than most of her peers. She was skilled socially, and, as it turns out, was always one to take control.

Diane told me at one point that the moms in the neighborhood in which she had grown up had nicknamed her *comandante,* meaning commander. I would come to learn that the nickname was an early indication of controlling personality traits which would continue to manifest themselves throughout our relationship.

My family consisted of Mom and Dad and five of us kids. My dad had grown up in a small coal town in the mountains of north-central Pennsylvania. He hadn't gone to college, and he relocated to New Jersey to find a job. My mom had grown up in southern New Jersey in the same house in which my siblings and I eventually were raised. She had attended college for a short time but didn't graduate. Eventually, she took a job at the same company as my dad. Not long afterwards, I was born.

Looking back, my fundamental focus around the time I met Diane was my interest in being a father. I have always loved kids and saw myself being a dad to at least three or four of my own. Diane was interested in a family as well. After a year and half together we were both eager and ready to be married and become parents.

Laurie was literally a honeymoon baby. Diane and I married in June, and Laurie was born in late February.

I still remember the day of her birth vividly: the excitement, the fear, the pride—all of it. I couldn't have been happier.

Given the way I'd been able to make a living, I had flexibility during the week that enabled me to spend lots of time being a dad. I rarely worked more than thirty hours a week, and therefore I was one of the few dads able to be at most of our girls' daytime school functions and activities. The fact that Diane and I were usually together at these events created a very favorable impression for teachers and other parents regarding our commitment to our girls. I took great pride in that.

After a year or so, we started discussing having another child. At that point, we both had an interest in at least three kids, and possibly more. It was nice to be in sync regarding such a fundamental family issue. Given how easily and quickly we were able to have Laurie, it didn't occur to us that having more children would be an issue. By the time another year went by, however, we started to wonder if something was wrong. After all the standard infertility tests and drug treatments, and a particularly horrible ectopic pregnancy experience, we were told that in vitro fertilization was our only natural option. We decided it was an option we would pursue only once, after which we would happily accept parenting Laurie if the procedure failed.

After much stress and consternation, we were extremely pleased to have the in vitro process go well and were particularly happy to have another daughter. Brooke seemed like a miracle at that point, and

I couldn't have been happier to be the father of two daughters.

I don't imagine too many couples are able to navigate the childbearing and parenting processes in perfect harmony. We didn't either, but looking back on our time together, I think we did a fairly admirable job.

I certainly don't look back now and regret having our two daughters. They brought me the most joy I've ever experienced, and all the best memories I have involve them. After their births, I truly loved being around for them, and especially telling them I loved them and hearing it in return.

Chapter 2

From Happy to Empty

Our time together as a family in New Jersey was fairly happy. Before Laurie turned one year old, Diane had stopped working in order to be a stay-at-home mom. This was a decision I supported, and I was doing well enough financially to make Diane's being a full-time mother a comfortable option for the family.

My relationship with Diane was a bit of a different story. I noticed she had become increasingly status-conscious, and she insisted we join a local country club. She claimed she had no social circle given that most women in the general neighborhood had full-time jobs. Her rationale was that women who were members of the club were more likely to be home during the day in order to socialize and arrange play dates for the kids. In hindsight, it was around this time that I began to perceive a decidedly vain side to her. Driving an upscale vehicle was now a must for her (she announced she would never, ever, drive a minivan….an interesting stance for a stay-at-home mom). Within the circle of friends she developed, many had second homes and housecleaners (and unlike Diane, had college degrees). We now started traveling to the Outer Banks for two weeks each summer (bringing her parents along), a family tradition we enjoyed for ten years.

Diane was always very social, and that was a trait that I honestly admired, but Diane loved to go to parties and was able to drink for hours at a time. It seemed there wasn't a party she didn't want to attend—or one she wanted to leave. By contrast, I'd never been a big drinker. I certainly wasn't a teetotaler, and I never judged anyone who could drink responsibly while maintaining a reasonable level of social etiquette. But I think it's important for one to realize when college days are over and the increased responsibility to exercise self-control. I recognized that my inclination to have no more than a drink or two made it easier for me to not overindulge. I knew that handling alcohol was a struggle for many people, and I never lost sight of the fact that I was pretty lucky not to feel any compulsion to overdrink. I was particularly proud to be recognized by our social circle as a reliable designated driver.

I've tried to look back and make an honest and objective assessment of who I was as a person during this timeframe. Was I a good dad? Was I a good husband? Was I a good provider for the family? I'm comfortable in thinking I was. We had two great daughters and what seemed to be a functional family structure. I was always around for the family. I occasionally played golf when the girls where in school, and we had a nice social group of people who we regularly spent time with. Being the sole financial support for my family made me feel particularly proud.

I did come to some very important insights around this time, however. I was observing more and more ways in which Diane and I were fundamentally different. My greatest concern was that I had begun to chafe under her controlling nature. And her need for attention and constant efforts to impress people started to create tension between us. At first I thought that what I came to call her pretentiousness was fundamental insecurity due to her lack of a college education. But I increasingly realized that she was purposely putting herself into the social path of women who had possessions and a certain lifestyle she wanted. It was something much more than insecurity, although I wasn't sure of its exact nature. All I really knew was that, whatever it was, I didn't like it.

One thing I knew for sure, however, was that I loved being a family. My identity was first and foremost that of a dad. Everything else I did in life took a backseat to being a good father. In my wallet I still had a piece of paper on which I had written down three goals for myself shortly after Diane and I were married: 1) Be a great Dad; 2) Be a faithful husband; and 3) Never get divorced. I was proud at the time that I had been true to all three goals, and I remained focused on continuing to achieve all of them in the long run.

I must say that I always felt Diane was a good mom. She truly cared for the girls as much as I did, and I think it was this fact that enabled me to still enjoy being together as a family unit.

An ominous change for our family came when I accepted a professional opportunity with one of my clients in central Pennsylvania. Living in central New Jersey had been an enjoyable experience, but the cost of living and general materialism in that area began to feel unseemly. When Brooke was about to enter kindergarten, and with Laurie heading into middle school, it seemed like the least disruptive time for us to move.

We sold our house in New Jersey at the top of the real estate market—a lucky break—and bought a very nice house in a wooded neighborhood in central Pennsylvania. The girls entered school, and we settled into a healthy family routine that seemed to validate our decision to move. Laurie enjoyed riding horses, an activity she'd begun in New Jersey after a horse farm was developed close to our neighborhood. She truly loved being around horses, and I was exceedingly proud of the way she conquered her fear of riding to eventually become an accomplished equestrian.

Not long after moving to Pennsylvania, we decided to reward Laurie's dedication to horses by enabling her to purchase a horse of her own. Horses are not cheap in any respect, especially with the cost of boarding, vet bills, and other expenses, but I knew that Laurie would be dedicated to the responsibilities of horse ownership. I also felt that her being accountable for the management of different activities that were required to properly develop as a rider, as well as care for a horse, could provide discipline that might benefit her throughout life. Watching Laurie develop as a rider, compete successfully in shows, and genuinely love horses was one of the most special experiences I've ever had. I was truly proud of her.

The ominous aspect came within a year or so of our arrival in Pennsylvania when Diane met a couple of women whose influence changed my relationship with Diane and disrupted our family forever. This is not to say that they can be held directly responsible for anything other than their own inappropriate behavior, but their friendship with Diane opened up doors to a party world that she was very willing and ready to walk through.

The best way for me to describe these two women, Sheila and Linda, is as very sexually charged and inappropriate. Both were married. It was not long after Diane met Sheila and Linda that she started going out for dinner and drinks with them on a regular basis. I didn't initially object to her going out since I knew she loved a good time, and I was more than happy to stay home with the girls. That's not to say that Diane and I didn't go out together on a regular basis as well. We routinely went out together for dinner and a couple drinks. I enjoyed going with her to movies or to see a band after dinner. Now that Laurie was old enough to babysit for herself and Brooke, we increasingly had freedom to spend time together as a couple.

But Sheila and Linda were a problem. It was not long before stories surfaced regarding the type of activities they enjoyed. Examples of stories that I remember include an evening at Linda's house with a couple of her female friends present, including Sheila. Someone thought it would be fun to blindfold Linda's husband Bruce and have Linda and two of her girlfriends drop their pants so that Bruce could feel their buttocks in order to identify each woman. We were also told of a night out when Sheila and Linda took their husbands and several couples to a concert. They all stayed in a hotel afterwards, and the story indicated that many of them rolled around, mostly naked, with each other in one of the hotel rooms. A similar story involved a party at Linda's house during which one of the men in attendance ended up performing oral sex on his wife in full view of everyone outside near the pool.

I understand that people have the right to enjoy whatever fun they want in their own private settings. And I've heard of swingers who engage in fringe behavior. I'm not a prude, but neither am I interested in enjoying that type of group fun. What concerned me, however, was that Diane didn't seem bothered by these stories. In fact, she seemed intrigued, which made me a bit nervous. I also became uncomfortable socializing with these women and their husbands, knowing of these salacious details.

I had hoped, even expected, that Diane would be just as surprised and appalled as I was upon hearing these stories. But the opposite seemed true as she continued to grow closer to both Sheila and Linda and spent longer periods of time with both of them. Their nights out together grew later and later, with Diane routinely coming home after midnight.

Another negative development was the increase in Diane's controlling behavior. As our girls grew older, she seemed intent on exerting increasing control over all areas of their lives. For example, she insisted on being the only one to help the girls with their homework and made sure she was involved in all aspects of decision-making, no matter how minor.

I was still able to be home regularly in order to be a helpful dad. This made Diane's life quite a bit easier, especially when Laurie needed to be taken to the horse farm. I would often take her to the farm in order to enable Diane to be involved in whatever Brooke may have had scheduled at that time. As a result, Diane needed to juggle less then she would have otherwise had I not been available. Given that she was a stay-at-home mom to begin with, I felt she was enjoying opportunities with our daughters that many women who work outside the home routinely miss out on. But I also felt privileged to be so involved in my daughters' lives and activities.

I could sense, however, that Diane was feeling more and more entitled and was focusing more attention on her relationship and activities with Sheila and Linda. She would go out with them several times a month. It started to bother me that she would normally leave to go out with them around six in the evening, and I therefore started to wonder why she needed to be out so late. And just where were they for that long? In light of the stories I had heard, it made me uneasy.

A major turning point for the worse came when Diane announced that she would like to go away for a girls only vacation with Sheila and Linda. They had hatched a plan go to Puerto Vallarta, Mexico for a week. They eventually invited a fourth woman, Shelly, along as well. Shelly was married to a man I had gotten to know and respect in the neighborhood, and I actually felt that having her along would be helpful. I hoped she'd serve to be somewhat of a calming influence. In hindsight, it's amazing how uncomfortable I was with the dynamic that was forming between the three of them.

People within our social circle had remarked at the seeming decadence of a stay-at-home mom going on a girls only vacation for a week. Given that I could arrange my schedule to accommodate it, however, and believing that having Diane gone for a week would give me the opportunity to interact with the girls without the controlling tension Diane created, I never considered asking her not to go. I didn't feel it was my place to stop her since I wanted to avoid acting as controlling as she had become. Little did I know, however, how deeply this trip would undermine the basic trust and foundation of our relationship.

On a good note, a source of immense pride for me occurred at this time. Brooke was now in second grade at the Catholic school she attended. One day she came home with an envelope addressed to me. She and her classmates had been given an assignment that day to practice their cursive writing skills by writing about "the best person I know." Her teacher had thankfully made sure I saw what Brooke had written:

"The best person I know is: My Dad. He's always happy and cheerful. He cheers me up whenever I'm not happy. He always asks me to do something he thinks is fun. I love him very much"

I consider this note (which I will keep forever) to be one of my greatest achievements.

Chapter 3

Inappropriate Behavior

Diane was amazingly giddy as the date of her trip approached. I was both surprised and dismayed at the number of hours she spent on the computer, day and night, making plans, arrangements, and sending what seemed like endless emails. I say dismayed because one of my pet peeves regarding Diane's particular pattern of controlling behavior was the way she would chide me for the few times I needed to have a conference call in the evening with a client in another time zone. Even though I had likely been home since the girls had come home from school, and likely played outside with Brooke or took Laurie to the horse farm, she would spin my thirty-minute call into an act of child abandonment. The irony of her criticism, however, wasn't lost on me since Diane was now spending hours upon hours planning to leave me and the girls for a week for her own selfish pleasure. Diane was increasingly becoming a poster girl for double standards.

Knowing the sexually charged nature of both Sheila and Linda, I was becoming increasingly uncomfortable as their trip approached. I had conversations with Diane concerning my apprehensions of just what the three of them would feel free to do with total unaccountability during an entire week out of the country. Even so, I was outwardly as supportive as I could be. I had become so sensitive to her obsessive control that I would consciously avoid acting in any way that made me feel like I was modeling her.

I vividly remember her leaving the bedroom at three in the morning to get to the airport in time for their flight to Mexico. Although I was looking forward to spending time alone for a week with the girls, I started to wonder what Diane's reaction would be if I were the one leaving for a "boys only" vacation with men who had consistently exhibited a wild side. Although being away from Diane and the girls for a week didn't interest me, it was the double standard of her behavior that continued to eat at me.

Thankfully, the week with the girls went well. We kept busy, and I admit we ate some meals that most likely weren't high on anyone's nutritional list, but we had fun. I remember that Diane called home three times to talk to the girls and me during the week. Everyone was happy and fine, and Diane said she and the ladies were spending lots of time on the beach.

Diane returned home without any significant delays or travel issues, and I'll admit I was looking forward to seeing her. Being with the girls alone had been very rewarding and enjoyable, but I had come accustomed to being a family of four. One interesting thing I noticed was how easily the girls had acclimated to my role as primary caretaker. Even after Diane was back from Mexico for a couple of days, they would still ask me for help or information that they typically would have sought from Diane. I remember thinking that there was some dynamic operating with our girls (and maybe with all children) that clearly was a function of the aggregate time they spent with a parent. Nothing had changed other than they had gotten used to coming to me for an entire week.

Diane arrived back home late on a Saturday afternoon. That evening in bed she showed me the 'present' she'd brought home for me, a temporary "tramp stamp" tattoo on her back. Frankly, I don't remember what the tattoo depicted, but I do remember thinking that she knew I didn't like tattoos. For the next several days the tattoo served to remind me of the negative influence of Sheila and Linda.

I hadn't given a thought to what I expected from Diane when she returned from her vacation. I assumed she'd be rested, energetic, and appreciative to have had time away with her friends. I was completely taken aback the next afternoon when she simply couldn't stay awake. I noticed her sleeping on the couch early that Sunday afternoon and felt a significant level of annoyance. The flight back from Mexico to Pennsylvania wasn't an arduous one, and after a week of sitting on a beach, how tired could one be? Even so, wouldn't one feel some responsibility to stay awake and enjoy the family she hadn't seen in several days?

It was a few days later that I started to get answers to my questions. I received a call from the husband of the fourth friend, Shelly, who went on the trip with the other ladies. He discreetly told me how appalled Shelly was at the behavior of Diane, Sheila, and Linda. He related that the women were constantly involved in inappropriate behavior with other men, including being out in bars each night until 3 a.m. or later. I was told that they would drink and "interact" with men on the beach during the day and then make plans to meet them in a bar later that night. According to her husband, Shelly said she would never consider going on a vacation with Diane and her friends again.

Although I needed to confront Diane to at least give her a chance to respond to the information I'd been given, I knew deep down that it was likely true. It certainly explained Diane's extreme fatigue, and given the fears I had expressed before she left regarding the inappropriate behavior of Sheila and Linda, her lethargy now made perfect sense. When I broached the subject with Diane that evening, she became very defensive and angry. Yes, she said, they'd been in bars every night, and she had had many opportunities to take advantage of offers men were making to her. Yes, she danced and accepted drinks, but she said nothing worse happened.

The worst aspect of her reaction, though, was the way she vehemently defended Sheila, Linda, and herself. It would have been bad enough had she at least feigned remorse, but she had obviously chosen sides. It was clear to me that she felt her bonds with Sheila and Linda were now stronger and more important than her marital bonds. Looking back, this was the moment at which our marriage was lost. I certainly didn't know it then, nor was I even thinking in those terms. All I knew was that I was hurt, angry, and felt extremely betrayed.

From that point forward, Diane's controlling nature became much worse, and her interest in going out with her friends became a priority. The more I expressed my displeasure with her association with Sheila and Linda, the more she defended them and accused me of trying to control her. Any argument I made about inappropriate marital behavior and skewed priorities became gasoline on the fire of her self-righteous attitude. Why, she would ask, didn't the husbands of Sheila and Linda have a problem with their behavior? "Oh," I'd respond, "you mean the guys who are feeling other women's asses and rolling around with barely-dressed people in hotel rooms?" She'd respond that I had no right to judge them. That became her standard retort.

Frankly, I felt I did have a right to judge them, especially since their wives were having a significant influence on my marriage. Also, we judge people and situations all the time, and justifiably so. Aren't there kids we deem as bad influences on our own children? Aren't there parents we feel don't provide proper oversight when our children are in their homes? We do judge, and frankly I think it's our duty to judge whether or not improper, unhealthy, or immoral behavior is impacting our relationships and loved ones.

It was around this time that Diane joined the local women's Bunco group, the members of which would spend an evening once a month at someone's home playing a mindless card game as an excuse to drink, gossip, and talk trash about their husbands. The host home would rotate, but it was always a source of aggravation for me when Bunco nights were hosted at our house. There were several things that bothered me about these gatherings. First, they were always held on Wednesday nights. That was not a problem for Diane since she didn't have to go to school or work the next day. Second, these evenings always started around 7 p.m. and were theoretically supposed to be over by 10 p.m. However, there was never a Bunco night at our house when there were not at least four or five women there until midnight. Third, the drunker these women got, the louder they became…..meaning that they got louder as the evening grew later.

Whenever Diane hosted a Bunco night at our home, I would have to lie on Brooke's bed with her starting at around 9:30 p.m. in order to help her tune out the noise of the raucous women so she could sleep. I never was on her bed for less than an hour given the increasing noise level. I can distinctly remember silently asking myself why I should be the one lying on Brooke's bed while my stay-at-home wife was getting drunker and louder downstairs, thus impeding our daughters' ability to get the sleep needed to ensure they were fresh and ready for school in the morning. I also had fleeting thoughts as to whether a group of loud, drunk men playing poker until midnight would be well-received at our house. Even though I had no interest in having men over to drink, I couldn't help recognizing that there was a significant double standard being applied yet again.

As Diane's "girls nights" continued, I noticed the way she dressed for them became increasingly provocative.

I remember a shopping spree she went on with some women in the neighborhood, after which she came home with the tightest, sexiest jeans I'd ever seen her wear. I honestly felt they were obscene for a mother of two daughters (one a teenager) to wear. After all, wasn't being a proper role model for her daughters one of her chief parental duties? When Diane tried on the jeans in our bedroom, I remember my reaction: "Wow, I sure hope those are just for me and only to be worn inside the house." Although I said it in an admiring way, I was honestly taken aback. Diane's reaction was to assure me the jeans were only to be worn as part of an ensemble that included a sweater that covered her buttocks, and she put the sweater on to show me.

A couple of weeks later she was getting ready to head out with her friends again and I noticed she was wearing the sexy jeans without the sweater. As it became obvious that she planned to go out dressed in such a manner, I asked her about the sweater. She reiterated that it was part of the jeans ensemble, but she immediately became angry and defensive, citing that she hadn't meant that the jeans would *always* be worn with the sweater. I asked her exactly who she was dressing for, or if she felt the need to dress in a sexy manner for Sheila and Linda? Were they trying to arouse each other, or was I missing something? To me it was bad enough that they would be out in a bar (or bars) until midnight, but to add the provocative clothes into the mix was another slap to me, and very disrespectful. Regardless, I'd begun to feel that married people shouldn't regularly be out in bars without their spouses as late as midnight. Nothing much good happens in bars that late, especially when your spouse is at home waiting for you.

Diane increasingly began to accuse me of trying to control her, and by this time I was increasingly convinced of my inability to trust her. I nevertheless was making an attempt to keep our family together. I asked some colleagues (women and men) if what I was tolerating with Diane was a red flag and whether I was being unreasonable. The feedback was emphatic and unanimous: they would never accept behavior such as Diane's from their spouses, nor would they expect their spouse to accept it.

Truthfully, I had known for several years at this point that I didn't love Diane anymore, but I still very much loved being a family together. I can honestly say that the girls didn't witness or sense any tension between us yet. I know many people feel that way when the truth would indicate otherwise, but I'm confident about this point. Unfortunately, that would not be the case later on.

Diane's behavior over the next year and a half has subsequently been described by counselors as psychologically abusive (towards me). The counselors are emphatic that I had been an enabler by continually acquiescing to Diane's increasingly inappropriate behavior, but I honestly had no interest in being a broken family. I loved being around the girls, and I was proud of the dad I was. Nothing mattered more to me than my children. As my marriage got worse, the joy I seemed to get from being with the girls increased. They were the result of our marriage, and I equated being with them with being married.

I should make it clear at this point that Diane and I would still frequently go out for dinner and drinks ourselves. I wanted to work on our relationship, and she clearly was becoming more interested in nights out. I figured that if we spent time out together she might have less of a need to be in the company of her friends so frequently.

A dilemma presented itself when Diane announced that she, Sheila, and Linda wanted to go away on another girls only vacation. This time they planned to go to the Dominican Republic for a week. I was flooded with different thoughts and emotions at the news. Did I really want to have her away again given that I honestly didn't trust her? Did she even deserve to go away again? It wasn't cheap, and this was money we could use for better purposes, like college savings or even a family vacation.

We had several long discussions about it. I finally told her I wasn't going to stop her from going if she truly wanted to, but I made it very clear that by supporting her vacation plans I wasn't also condoning her being in bars every night or interacting inappropriately with other men. I was fine with a girls only vacation as long as it was 'girls only'. This was my attempt at regaining some level of trust, which I knew I needed in order to make our marriage better. Diane professed her absolute understanding of my position and wholeheartedly agreed to act appropriately. My friends, however, thought I was crazy.

One thing I absolutely understand now is how a spouse's purposeful pattern of undermining trust is a form of psychological abuse that becomes debilitating over time. I started feeling acutely abused during the time Diane was away for the second time. I found myself waking up every night between 2 a.m. and 3 a.m., feeling sick and confused. Why was I enabling her to cause me such psychological trauma? Why did our marriage mean so much to me and apparently so little to her?

It turns out that my friends were right. Once again Diane displayed exhaustion upon returning, and this time she was defiant. After several sleepless nights ruminating about why I was accepting this behavior, my patience had run out. After I pointed out that she didn't seem to have gotten much sleep on her trip, she recounted in detail her interaction with a man from Austria who had made his desire for a romance very clear to her. Her self-righteous attitude and posture of entitlement made me sick. Her body language implied that I was lucky that she had even decided to return to me given the other options that had presented themselves. When I considered that we had spent family funds for a second time for her to selfishly go away, only to return with the attitude that she had done me a favor by restraining herself from worse adulterous behavior, I hit rock bottom. I felt like I was in quicksand, with every effort to free myself causing me sink that much faster.

Sadly, there were several other abusive situations over the next year or so, including:

- Diane and I had attended my high school reunion. Her flirtation with a man there was so flagrant that the wife of a good friend of mine discreetly approached me and said, "you better keep an eye on your wife."

- Diane and I went out to dinner and later decided to have a couple of drinks and see a band that she liked. It was very obvious that Diane was openly flirting with the guitar player, who had no qualms about returning her attention. The band played a song called "Crazy Bitch," which ends with the lyrics "You're crazy, but I love the way you fuck me." Diane pointed to the guitar player as she sang those words, and he gave her a broad smile in return. I stood there, completely numb and nauseous at what had just taken place. It truly seemed like she was now purposely pushing me to the point of divorcing her.

- Diane and I took a trip together to Jamaica to work on our relationship. (She obviously had plenty of trips and vacations during our marriage.) We met a couple of men there who said they were in the "male entertainment" business (as in Chippendales). Diane was intrigued. During our conversation, one of the men gave Diane a business card. After saying goodbye, she and I walked back to our chairs. As we were walking, Diane stuck the business card in the waistband of her bikini bottom so that most of the card was sticking out the top of the band. When we arrived at our chairs, I said that I was going to take a walk and said she was welcome to come along. I assumed that she had forgotten about the card sticking out of her bikini, so I asked her to throw it away. She ignored me and started to walk down the beach as if she intended to walk with her husband with a male entertainment business card in her bikini. After I repeated the request, it became obvious that she had no intention of removing the card. I grabbed the card and tore it to pieces. At that point, I truly began to wonder if she might be mentally ill.

The final straw for me came shortly thereafter and again involved Sheila and Linda. The occasion was a girls only birthday party, hosted at Linda's, for a female acquaintance of the ladies. I figured that this was a setting that might not lend itself to wholesome activity, and I requested that Diane drive herself to the party with the expectation that, should things become inappropriate, she could (and should) drive herself home. She agreed that this was acceptable. On the day of the party, however, she announced she was going to ride along with Sheila since she didn't want to be concerned about drinking and driving.

Frankly, I was tired of being told things would be different going forward. I wanted to see for myself just how these women acted when left to their own plans. I expected that, since it was summer, the party would be held around the pool on the back patio.

Since Laurie was home and available to sit for Brooke, I told the girls that I needed to go out for a little while and that I'd be home before their bedtimes. I drove to Linda's neighborhood and parked down the street. I had no intention of trespassing or making a scene, so I walked along the edge of the neighbor's property. I could hear raucous laughter, and the party sounded like it was in full swing. I could see women sitting in chairs arranged in a semi-circle on the patio. I could also see two male strippers, both wearing nothing but a sock on their genitals. As one of the strippers gave each woman a lap dance, the other was in the middle of the patio performing a lewd and provocative dance. After a few minutes, I saw Diane walk towards the dancing stripper and dance in what can only be described as a pornographic manner. She put her face within an inch or so of the stripper's genitals as she danced. All the blood seemed to drain from my body. I was totally numb.

Eventually, one of the strippers left, and the other one sat by the pool as the women (all married) went inside to put on bikinis. They all then proceeded to get into the hot tub with the remaining stripper, and I witnessed several women take off their tops and make out with the stripper. I couldn't see the faces of the women or identify anyone in particular, but it didn't matter to me anymore.

Things weren't going to get better between me and Diane.

Chapter 4

Counseling & Divorce

I knew at this point that I did not want to live with Diane anymore. By the same token, I also knew I didn't want to breakup up the family and likely spend the majority of my time away from the girls (a subject that will be addressed later.) It would be hard for me to overstate the emotional turmoil I was experiencing. The girls were still the focus and joy of my life. I knew Laurie would be heading to college in a couple years, and I wanted to provide as much stability in their lives as possible. Brooke was heading to middle school and would still be glad to have dad around for the next few years. I enjoyed spending time with her and her friends, ice skating, bike riding, playing basketball, and other activities. These were great times. I loved the fact that Brooke would look to me to be with them at such times and to have me facilitate their plans.

When considering the reality of divorce, I recognized the significant dilemma I was in. Diane had no college education, nor had she gained any work experience over the past fifteen years. Divorce was not going to be kind to me. I wasn't as concerned about the financial ramifications, but given the lifestyle I had created for our family, it was going to be incumbent upon me to provide similar environments for what essentially would become two households. I knew this meant that I'd need to ramp up my work activities in order to generate extra income. I figured I was going to see the girls less than half the time since I'd be traveling frequently, and the divorce court would almost surely side with Diane on the custody issue. When I contemplated how much I enjoyed being with the girls every day, the thought of becoming a part-time dad and seeing them less than half of the time was truly gut-wrenching.

My stress level skyrocketed. I reflected constantly on the horrible choice I seemed to have: continue to live with a wife I had come to despise or lose my daily role of being a dad to the girls I loved so much.

I decided to keep the family together if at all possible. I told Diane that I felt we needed to go to marriage counseling if we expected anything to change for the better. I was honest with her that my trust level for her was close to zero and that it wasn't going to change without some significant effort and commitment on both our parts. She agreed to try and work things out through counseling. I wasn't under any delusions that I would fall madly in love with her, but I hoped to make things good enough to continue to be a functioning family unit. I told Diane that she could feel free to choose the counselor, and she said she'd prefer a woman. It really didn't matter to me who we saw, as long as we both made an honest effort.

Our counseling efforts can be summarized as mostly fruitless. I was hoping that the counselor would tell Diane that she was damn lucky to be a stay-at-home mom at a time when most women needed to be employed full-time *and* be a mom. I expected any reputable counselor to explore Diane's discontent with a life filled with lunches, girlfriends, and numerous vacations. Finally, I hoped that her inappropriate sexually-charged behavior with other men, including the male strippers, would be appropriately addressed.

I was honest with the counselor about my lack of trust, which she thankfully said she completely understood based on the lurid summary of Diane's vacations and parties with her friends. I also said that, despite some role model issues concerning our girls, Diane was an attentive mom, which I honestly meant. I never felt we weren't good parents, which was a big factor in my attempt to keep the family together through counseling.

One revelation during the counseling was Diane's insistence that she wasn't having as much fun in her life as she would like. When she first blurted out this assertion, I wasn't sure I had heard her correctly. She hadn't previously made any such claim. Even the counselor seemed confused and asked Diane to repeat herself. Any real hope I had of keeping the family together ended at that moment. I already felt that too much of her attention and activities, as well as our family resources, were being directed towards her quest for fun and pleasure. If she truly felt she deserved more (whatever that might have meant), then I didn't see any way I could compromise. The counselor did not see how she could help us find common ground.

We went to two more counseling sessions, but there was simply no path to take. It was clear that our priorities were entirely different. One valuable aspect of our counseling is that it provided a forum for me to emphasize (and Diane to acknowledge) that I had been entirely faithful to her for the seventeen years of our marriage. I took the issue of fidelity seriously, and I never came close to being unfaithful. It wasn't an issue of getting caught. I simply didn't want to fail my family.

As it became clear that separating was a likely reality in the very near future, I felt like I *was* failing my family, and this thought kept me up at night. I routinely woke up at three or four in the morning and lay awake, wondering how things had gotten to this point and how I was going to deal with not seeing the girls on a daily basis. Then the anger set in. How could Diane be so damn selfish? It bothered me greatly that she was going to be with the girls much more often than I was. What had I done to deserve that? I was the one at home with the girls while she was out in bars or out of the country. I started thinking that I should have insisted she seek employment, at least part-time, as a way of redirecting her energy away from inappropriate behavior. Maybe that dose of reality would have made her appreciate the significant free time she had enjoyed for so long. What I didn't understand yet though was just how bad things were going to get and just how impossible a situation I was actually in.

Once I finally told Diane I wanted a divorce, her demands started almost immediately. She had gone to see an attorney and knew there was significant leverage on her side. I was in no mood to fight since I had entered what was a significant state of depression. I even went to see a doctor but balked at taking any medication. I decided I would muddle through it all by focusing on doing the right thing for the girls. But it was hard to listen to Diane spew her venom about what she could get if we went to court and that I better not underestimate how strong a person she was.

It was then that I started making a series of mistakes that radically affected the next several years of my life. What I've learned is that mistakes tend to lead to a loss of control. In turn, a loss of control tends to lead to feelings of frustration, and frustration leads to anger, which results in the likelihood of making additional mistakes. It's about as vicious as cycles get.

My first mistake was that I decided to agree to a separation agreement (a post-nuptial agreement) within sixty days. I didn't want to have the girls notice the increasing tension between us any more than necessary. Diane had become like a shark sensing blood in the water. The circling had started, and the water was starting to churn. The anger I harbored towards her was tempered only by the depression I felt at the thought of telling the girls we were separating, as well as the inevitable reality of seeing much less of them. I was also committed to minimizing attorney fees. I felt strongly that any available money would be better used to benefit the girls, such as college savings funds, rather than for legal bickering. This turned out to be mistake number two. There is nothing wrong with minimizing attorney fees in a divorce, and, in fact, it's a very worthwhile goal, but only if both sides are committed to that goal. If your spouse is committed to exploiting you in every way possible, then all you're doing by trying to save legal fees is letting your guard down at the very time you likely need the most protection.

Essentially, I was fighting a dragon with a dull sword and one arm tied behind my back. At the time, I was consumed by the guilt I felt from the thought of our girls becoming children of a broken home. I could have benefited from seeing a counselor during this period to gain some perspective on why I was shouldering the blame for things I couldn't control. Being a good dad and faithful husband were totally within my control, but having a good marriage takes the commitment of two people. I'm not saying I didn't make mistakes during our marriage, but I eventually realized that shouldering the majority of the blame internally wasn't healthy or justified.

The first issue we dealt with was the house. It was obvious to both of us that Diane would not be able to afford to stay there with the girls given the costs necessary to maintain it. It was a fairly large home on a wooded lot with extensive landscaping. I normally cut the lawn, and generally took care of the property myself. So the first decision I made was to buy her out of the house and stay there myself instead of selling it, which likely would have taken many months given the real estate market at the time. Buying it myself would eliminate months of uncertainty regarding a potential sale and enable Diane to have cash within thirty days to find a place to stay. It would also give the girls a home that represented security and familiarity when they were with me. Diane also benefited from a seemingly above-market appraisal which was used to determine the sixty-five percent of the equity I had agreed to give her.

Beyond that, I agreed to give her sixty percent of the assets we had accumulated and also agreed to pay hundreds of dollars more in child support than the (state) required amount. I also agreed to pay her $1700 in alimony each month for up to 10 years (unless she cohabitated or remarried) and to pay one hundred percent of the girls private school tuition, one hundred percent of the girls' health insurance, and all of Laurie's auto insurance costs through college. In short, I was extremely generous. I knew I didn't need to pay this much, but I was consumed by guilt. Just as importantly, I hoped that by being more than fair to Diane, she would recognize my attempt to make things as comfortable for her and the girls as possible and would react over time with some level of appreciation, or at least reduced rancor.

The financial reality of separating was sobering for me though. I calculated that in order to pay alimony, child support, private school tuition for both girls (Catholic school), health insurance for the girls, auto insurance for Laurie, etc. I would need to earn over $80,000 (before taxes) just to cover these expenses. That was before I earned the dollars I needed to pay for the house, food, and my other living expenses. I learned that there's a fine line between being generous and being stupid.

One additional issue regarding the separation agreement needs to be highlighted since it became a source of significant aggravation to me. During the marriage I opened 529 College Savings Plans in my name for each of the girls. By the time Diane and I separated, I had accumulated approximately $110,000 in <u>each</u> of the plans. I knew, however, that these sums, though substantial, would not be enough to pay for as much of their college as I'd hoped. I therefore decided to place another $30,000 in my plan for Laurie (my professional financial planner designation made me well qualified for such decisions). My intent was to roll over any leftover funds to Brooke's plan upon Laurie's college graduation. But once Diane and her attorney noticed the deposit into Laurie's college plan, they insisted that the separation agreement include a clause enabling Diane to withdraw $18,000 ($30,000 x 60%) for her own use should she choose. Less than sixty days later, Diane withdrew $18,000, literally taking part of our daughters' college savings for herself. I doubt I'll ever get over that.

  The separation agreement also specified that I would have legal custody of the girls on Tuesday and Thursday evenings and every other weekend, as well as the customary sharing of holidays. This was a standard schedule for a father in my circumstances of being the primary financial support for the family. But it was also stated that I could have the girls at any other time that was mutually agreeable. I put too much stock in this clause since I assumed there would be times when Diane would be 'mutually agreeable '. Not getting a separate legal custody agreement at the time of our separation was yet another one of my mistakes. I didn't pursue a custody agreement because I continued to focus on avoiding unnecessary legal fees, and I assumed having our custody arrangement spelled out in our legal separation agreement was sufficient. In fact, the vast majority of the divorced people we knew didn't have, or need, even as much detail as we had in writing. If two people are cooperative and trustworthy, it's not necessarily a problem to keep a healthy amount of flexibility in custody arrangements, which usually benefits everyone, especially the kids. But the less cooperation provided by at least one of the divorcing spouses, the more critical it is to keep things legally buttoned-up and enforceable. The tricky part is that attitudes and intentions can change as circumstances change (especially when significant others on one or both sides appear).

I found the adjustment to living alone without the girls every bit as hard as I feared. Watching them drive away after a visit was tortuous. To make matters worse, I had to really focus on increasing my income to handle the significant increase in living expenses. I knew I had been generous to Diane for the right reasons, but it was a stressful reality nonetheless. And as a result, I needed to miss some of my weekday evenings with the girls due to business travel. It was a sobering reality and a harbinger of difficult times ahead.

One thing that I requested of Diane is that we agree on not introducing any significant other to the girls within the first year of our family separation (which was not something legally enforceable or even able to be legally documented). Obviously, we were both free to date, but according to a couple of family counseling books I'd read about divorce issues, involving the kids too quickly in a new relationship was a fairly common mistake to avoid. Kids need time to adjust. And both parents typically need more time to adjust to being divorced than they may realize.

Chapter 5

Lies & Dysfunctional Behavior

Diane bought a townhouse in a neighborhood within two miles of where we had all lived together. It was an upscale development and relatively expensive for the area. It was clear to me that she extended herself financially to an uncomfortable degree given that she had no job at that point and no reason to be overly confident of generating significant income in the near future given her lack of recent work experience. But as I would come to learn, this fit Diane's pattern perfectly. She wasn't going to let divorce and the lack of a job get in the way of the lifestyle she felt she deserved.

Within a short time Diane was sending the girls over with bills they were told I needed to pay. Some bills were for activities the girls were involved in that I knew nothing about and for which I therefore had no input. Other bills were for auto repairs and maintenance that were simply not my responsibility. The worst part was that the girls were being told by Diane that the financial support I paid her each month was for basic expenses and that I was still obligated to pay for other things as well. This was, of course, pure fabrication and a hurtful piece of disinformation. Indeed, it was not information that should have been a topic of discussion with the girls in the first place. As I was soon to discover, though, this was just the beginning of a very conscious effort on Diane's part to pull the girls away from me and to create a new family environment that I was expected to financially subsidize, but be alienated from entirely.

Before Diane moved into her townhouse, she struck up a relationship with a man who she said she met one Friday night while out with her girlfriends. Dave had moved to central Pennsylvania about two years earlier after retiring from the CIA. Although I didn't know it at the time, I had actually met Dave about a year earlier when I was introduced to him by the woman who was the realtor we had worked with in purchasing our home. Ironically, we'd met in a jewelry store where I had purchased a Pandora bracelet for Diane's upcoming birthday. Diane and Dave were now dating.

Over the next couple of months, Diane and Dave started to date more seriously. I was frankly concerned that Diane was becoming involved in a serious relationship only a couple of months removed from our twenty-year relationship (including the time we dated). She certainly had the right to date, but I couldn't help become a bit uncomfortable when the girls started to mention Dave. I may have been naïve in thinking that Diane would honor our agreement to keep the girls away from significant others for a reasonable period of time, but I truly felt that she would make sure there was a healthy transition period for them. I couldn't have been more wrong. This is when my living hell began.

Dave, it turns out, had been divorced for many years and was the father of three daughters. By his own admission, he was an absentee father who had travelled nine months a year for his job. In that way, he couldn't have been more unlike me. Whereas I had limited my working hours to be available for my children, he admitted that he was never there for his girls. Although I had no choice in the matter, he certainly wasn't the type of man I'd hoped would be spending time with my girls. Shortly afterwards, no more than four or five months from the time Diane had moved, Dave started sleeping over once or twice a week at the townhouse. It apparently didn't matter whether the girls were there or not.

It should have come as no surprise that a woman who disrespected me in so many ways while we were married would act inappropriately after we were divorced. I had given her too much credit by hoping she would begin to show greater restraint. I simply didn't realize the dysfunction I was dealing with at that point and how the divorce would initiate an almost sociopathic effort on her part to control the girls and make me irrelevant to their lives. Looking back, Dave was the main ingredient she needed to complete this objective, giving her the confidence to alienate me from my children. She started telling the girls that she had moved on and that I needed to move on as well. Unbelievably, the girls would come over to my house and parrot that exact wording to me. I was entirely taken aback. It had been only six months since we'd lived under the same roof as a family, but now my girls were telling me that I needed to move on. What was that supposed to mean? Move on from *what*? And why was it any business of the girls to be telling me what I should be doing as both a grown man and their father? To be clear, it wasn't a matter of my girls coming over and telling me that they loved me and hoped I would find a special woman someday. They came over and told me that their mom had said she'd moved on and that I should as well. At this point it actually became harder and harder for me to look forward to seeing the girls given the way they were doing their mother's bidding. And the look in their eyes was increasingly different... like they had a secret I didn't know. My sense was that they were being manipulated to think of me as merely a means to an end (money). In this way they were becoming more like Diane.

It became very clear that, with Dave now in the picture, Diane had convinced my girls that they were now a new family and that I needed to move on in a similar manner. Just as disturbing, I noticed how little contact my girls were having with me apart from my custodial visitations with them. I received no phone calls and only abbreviated answers to my texts. I certainly wasn't getting any proactive or unexpected communication from either of them. Increasingly, it was as if I were being forgotten or ignored. It was only much later when a counselor made me aware of the existence of Parental Alienation Syndrome and the typical patterns associated with alienation efforts that I now realize Diane was employing. At the time, all I knew was that I felt sick from the change in the girl's attitude and behavior towards me.

It was another of my mistakes not to try to gain a better understanding of what was actually happening with the girls and to see a counselor earlier than I did. But it was another vicious circle: I didn't know because I had never heard of the syndrome. Still, it's always a mistake to see a significant change in your kids' attitudes and behavior in a divorce situation and not try to gain to a deeper understanding of what is happening through professional help for yourself and for your children. Another mistake I made was to express my frustration to the girls by showing displeasure regarding their comments about my alleged need to move on. Divorce is naturally fraught with opportunities for anger and resentment, and when your ex purposely tries to hurt your relationship with your kids in order to help achieve his or her objective of excessive control, it may seem almost impossible not to express anger to anyone within listening distance. But when it comes to your kids, it should be avoided. It took me much too long to understand this, and nothing I learned along the way is more important.

Now that Dave was involved in a family setting with my girls, things began to spiral downwards quickly. Given that he was retired and therefore home during the day, he essentially became a part-time nanny to the girls. More importantly, his constant availability gave Diane a resource to pull the girls even farther away from me. She had started working part-time as a receptionist and on certain days her schedule would conflict with Brooke's arrival home from school or her transportation needs for dance practice or other activities. Frequently I would be available to help in these situations and would have gladly embraced opportunities to see Brooke. Now that Diane could use Dave instead,

I was not notified of such opportunities to help my daughter. This served two very significant objectives for Diane: first, it eliminated any opportunities for my having extra interaction with the girls; and second, it provided additional bonding time for Dave and my daughters.

Shortly thereafter, Diane made her intentions very clear regarding her alienation efforts. The occasion was a weekend trip to Florida that Diane had arranged with Brooke to see some friends from our neighborhood who had recently moved there. Given that only Brooke would be going with her, Diane asked me if I would be willing to have Laurie stay at my house from Friday evening through Sunday dinner. I enthusiastically said that would be fine, although I had plans for a couple of hours that Friday evening and also needed to help a friend in New Jersey move some furniture into storage for a couple hours on Sunday afternoon. Otherwise, I would be around to keep Laurie company all weekend. By this time Laurie was seventeen years old and certainly did not require me to babysit her. In fact, we regularly relied on her the previous two or three years to babysit for Brooke, sometimes overnight. As anyone with a seventeen year old would understand, Laurie was happy to have a few hours of alone time.

The weekend went along fine. Laurie and I enjoyed our weekend together, and it was enjoyable to spend quality time alone talking with her. However, later that week I received the following email from Diane.

> Laurie told me that after you confirmed she could be with you this past weekend while I took Brooke to Florida, she was left alone

Friday night and Sunday afternoon. Just so you are not surprised when you hear of alternate plans: I will make other arrangements for the girls in the future for these rare times and *I will not ask you to co-parent nor offer you to spend any such time with our daughter(s) in my absence.* (Italics added)

I responded by reminding her that she was always happy to have me take care of them when she was partying inappropriately with her girlfriends (domestically and abroad). She replied as follows.

You were home then. That is true.

The above is an *exact* transcription of the email messages she sent me. Not only was she telling me that I wasn't, in her opinion, worthy of being an adequate parent in her absence, but that she would ensure in the future that I wouldn't get the chance to have additional time with the girls if she were busy. And given that she had 80% custody this was not insignificant. (She also then provided written confirmation of her inappropriate behavior). This email was infuriating to me. In fact, I started to consider the possibility that having Laurie stay with me that weekend was part of a plan Diane had made to find an excuse to inform me that she would keep the girls away from me from then on. It was clear to me that, given Dave's availability to be with the girls at any time, Diane was using this dynamic to push me increasingly out of the girls' lives. I felt that if she had any issues with my history as a dad, or with my current interaction with the girls, that she should have notified the family court and/or had a professional family counselor intervene (neither of which ever happened).

Sadly, Diane was frequently demonstrating poor parenting decisions when given the opportunity to choose between being home with the girls or having her party time. Two relevant examples I'm aware of are:

1. Diane went away for a wedding in New Jersey with Dave starting on a Friday evening. Brooke's birthday had been that week, and she was having a birthday party at Diane's townhome starting at 6 p.m. on Sunday evening. Diane told Brooke she would be home at 2 p.m. on Sunday to prepare for the party. Instead, Diane and Dave returned to the townhome at 5:35 p.m., only minutes before Brooke's party began. I know this to be true because I called Brooke to make sure she was okay, and she told me that her mother wasn't back yet and that she was alone in the townhome. I drove over to the townhome, and Brooke joined me in my car until Diane and Dave returned. Who was the responsible parent?

2. In the middle of a snowstorm I received a phone call from a friend (who didn't like Diane) saying that my girls were home alone while Diane was out partying with friends. At that point, there were several inches of snow on the ground, and the forecast was for heavy snow to continue. It was not acceptable to me that I was paying significant amounts of monthly child support to Diane for her to be irresponsible and leave the girls alone while she was likely out drinking and needing to drive home in such dangerous weather. I called Diane's cell phone and when she answered I could barely hear anything over the blaring music. I asked her if she knew how bad the weather was outside and

suggested she leave immediately to join the girls safely at home. Afterwards I sent her this email message:

The fact that you would be out drinking and then driving home in this snow storm shows how little you care about anything but your own fun. It shows how little you care about the girls that you would take chances like that. You need to grow up or get help.

I started seeing a family counselor to help me understand ways I might better interact with the girls. I also wanted to see if what I perceived as Diane's efforts to separate me from them was typical during divorce or instead was a continuation of her pattern of control and psychological abuse towards me. I distinctly remember how adamant the counselor was that Diane's decision to get into a serious relationship with Dave immediately after a marriage of seventeen years was both very unusual and potentially damaging to the girls. The counselor told me the most common rule for dating after divorce was to be alone one year for each of the four or five years you were married. This is supposed to give you time to get back to the "real you." The counselor provided additional information that I jotted down: the vast majority of women who get separated or divorced after at least ten years of marriage wait at least twelve to thirty-six months before dating anyone; they usually wait even longer before they introduce a new man into their kids' lives. Although I knew that people were different and that circumstances differed as well, I at least had some justification now for my feelings of concern and uneasiness.

More importantly, as the counselor and I spoke about my marriage to Diane, she said something that would eventually give me insight into my frustrating experiences and explain why I had been unable to get Diane to act more appropriately. She looked at me with a very sad and serious expression and said, "Unfortunately Richard, Diane fits the classic profile of a narcissist." She went on to draw many parallels between Diane's behavior both during and after our marriage with the standard behavior exhibited by people with Narcissistic Personality Disorder. It all made sense. The parallels were undeniable, even uncanny. Her need for control, the focus on her own fun, a lack of respect and empathy for me—it all fit. Interestingly, during our marriage and separation Diane was constantly telling me how 'strong' she was. And the girls now started making comments to me about 'how strong mom is'. Clearly Diane was now making similar statements to the girls. My counselor confirmed that Diane's need to make people aware of 'how strong she was' was an indication of emotional issues, and another factor confirming her narcissistic personality affliction. Was she proving her strength now by creating ways to 'punish me'? (I'll explore Narcissistic Personality Disorder in a later chapter.)

My immediate concern was how to protect the girls. I couldn't alter Diane's decision to bring Dave into the girls' lives, and my telling her she was a classic example of a narcissist wasn't going to help the situation in the least. I decided to send her an email suggesting she have the girls see a counselor.

> I have concerns about the girls I want to share. Statistics show that the vast majority of women

who get separated/divorced after at least 10 years of marriage take at least 12 – 36 months before dating anyone, and even longer before they introduce a new man into their kids' lives.

As you know, you found Dave before you and the girls moved out of the house, and you introduced him to them shortly thereafter. Any counselor will tell you that this is way too early to expect reasonable adjustment by the entire family to a new love interest.

Please consider paying for the girls to see a counselor so that they can have a better understanding of your need to date so soon, and what consideration you gave to how that would affect everyone's adjustment to new circumstances after the breakup of their family structure of 17 years.

I tried to address the issue in a sensitive way. I think got the point across without being overly nasty. Unfortunately, I never received any response. Narcissism, by itself, is not the type of disorder that I could claim was endangering the girls. I knew I was stymied, and I also realized for the first time that I simply couldn't expect Diane to act in anyone's best interest other than her own given that, as a narcissist, her main orientation was towards herself.

Diane's use of her relationship with Dave as a means of control and as a tool to alienate me from the girls became an increasing problem. Some of the ways were subtle, such as making sure his car was parked directly in front of the townhouse every time I went over to pick up the girls for my custody periods—a reminder to me that he was there and around the girls. Even worse, on several occasions, as Brook would walk down the front steps to get into my car, Diane would stand at the open door behind her and swivel her hips with her hand on the back of her head in a taunting dance. I knew what she was essentially saying by doing that: I've moved on and am in control, and there's nothing you can do about it. Unfortunately, she was right. It infuriated me further, which I now understand was the desired effect. It was yet more psychological abuse.

Of greater concern was the violation of my custody times. As Dave became more of a staple in my girls' life, Diane increased her efforts to use that dynamic to her advantage. It started innocently, with one or both of the girls contacting me to say that they had special plans arranged for a sleepover at someone's house or had a party to go to. As a parent to my daughters, I well understood the issues of sleepovers, parties, and the value of social interaction. My belief was that if someone was going to suffer (my missing time with them, or their missing important time with their friends), it should be the parent and not the child. I tried to be understanding and flexible, but it became an entirely different issue when Diane and Dave started to arrange weekend trips with the girls that precluded me from seeing the girls at my appointed times.

I vividly remember a weekend trip they took to Washington, DC with no consideration for my standard custody time. I was told that Dave took them to visit the White House, which he presumably was able to arrange due to his CIA background and connections. It was certainly a nice opportunity for the girls, but it was also done without my permission to miss my scheduled time with Brooke, and represented a continuing attempt to create a bond between Dave and the girls as well as a further opportunity to alienate me. I remember wondering if he had ever taken his own girls to the White House.

A few weeks later there was another weekend trip during my custody time, several days at a resort in central Virginia. I distinctly remember this because Brooke made me aware of the upcoming trip and told me she would like to go. It was a gut-wrenching experience because I could see Diane and Dave's emerging pattern of alienation. I was put in a horrible situation because I didn't want to disappoint Brooke, but I was not going to continue to let the girls spend additional time away from me in order to act like the family we used to be with someone else, namely Dave. As it was, I only saw the girls a few hours a week, and now Diane and Dave were conspiring to take even that away from me. Providing me optional times to see the girls to compensate for this lost time wasn't practical given my work schedule, as well as the girls' school and activities schedules. I told Brooke that I didn't want to hurt her in any way but that I looked forward to my time with her and didn't want to continue to miss seeing her. I told her I wanted to see her that weekend and suggested she ask her mom to arrange the trip for another time. Within the next day or so, I received a letter from Diane stating that the upcoming trip was already planned and that I was not to expect Brooke to be available for pick up on the weekend.

Now I was pissed. I was her father, and I expected to see my daughter at the appointed time. I had never impeded Diane's time with the girls. In fact, I was paying a lot of money in child support in order to facilitate Diane's ability to care for (and enjoy time with) the girls. It was getting to be too much. It particularly bothered me that given Dave's lack of involvement in his own girls' lives he likely didn't have the emotional capacity to empathize with my feelings, and my need to see my girls. Regardless though, he was well aware of my custody time on Sundays, and therefore was a willing participant in the violation of my custody time with Brooke.

While they were away on the trip I decided to go to the townhouse at my regular time to pick up Brooke. I hadn't agreed to miss my time with Brooke, and I felt I had every right to see her. I took along the copy of our separation agreement to verify that I was empowered with custody at that specified time. As expected, no one was home, so I called the police. I waited in my car outside Diane' townhouse for the officer to show up. The rest is documented in a letter from my attorney to Diane the following week.

> I am in receipt of your letter dated XXXXX, in which you outline your intent to violate the custody rights of Richard. Richard did not agree to forfeit his custody rights at that time. Richard went to pick up Brooke as usual. After waiting several minutes for her to appear, he had Officer XXXXX of the Township Police Department knock on your door to verify your violation. Also, you violated Richard's custody rights several weeks earlier on XXXXXXX without his permission or consent.
>
> As a minor, your daughter Brooke is not entitled to decide whether or not to follow

the custody arrangement. You are required to immediately cease supporting or encouraging Brooke's decisions in this regard.

In light of the circumstances, Richard and I have been discussing legal action against you. As we proceed, we will be requesting that you be ordered to reimburse Richard for his legal expenses given your current and previous violation of his custody rights.

My anger was starting to get the best of me. After years of psychological abuse by Diane, and now her continued efforts to control and hurt me, the stress started to wear me down. I never wanted the girls to suffer from their parents' joint failure to make their marriage work. Certainly my guilt overtook my judgment to some degree concerning the expenses I agreed to pay, but that was easier to live with emotionally than feeling as if I wasn't doing enough. Still, the stress and anger were building, and my dislike for Dave was getting stronger by the day.

When some friends from the area started to contact me to say that Diane was telling people around town that 'the girl's father is not involved in their lives' I finally snapped. Finally, all the stress took over. I honestly wish it hadn't, but I was like a good-natured dog that had been kicked and abused for many years. Sooner or later, the dog's reaction will turn from friendly acceptance to defensive anger. Maybe that sounds like an excuse, but it's true.

I parked my car and walked to Diane's front door. I proceeded to knock, and then bang, on the door loudly, requesting to speak with Dave. He finally opened the door. Without going into the house or touching or threatening anyone, I proceeded to tell Dave he had no right to participate in efforts to violate my custody times with my girls, that he had been a shitty dad himself, and that word around town was that he was a bit of a player with women. And I didn't say any of it in a friendly manner. After a minute or two, he instructed Diane to call the police. At that point I left. The incident marked the one and only time I ever set foot on Diane's property, but it was one too many. That moment sparked a series of events that ultimately gave Diane and Dave significant control over me. It was my worst mistake of many. Losing your temper is the one thing you need to fight against. In contentious divorce situations, with many emotional undercurrents involving your kids, money, and significant others, it can be extremely hard to keep emotionally contained. But it's important that you find a way to do it.

Chapter 6

Arrested

It wasn't long before Diane filed a restraining order against me. I knew it was coming, and frankly I felt horrible that I had lost my temper. In my first forty-nine years I had never been in any legal trouble. Other than a few speeding tickets, I'd never broken any laws. Legally, I still hadn't broken any law. What I didn't realize at the time (and had no way of knowing) was that I was about to give my control-freak ex-wife nearly total control over me.

The restraining order process involves a temporary order being issued at the time a complaint is filed. Unfortunately, there's very little proof required (is it fabricated?), and no way for a person to contest a temporary order. Then a court date is set within a few weeks for a judge to determine if a permanent order will be issued, and if so, for how long and with what provisions or restrictions. This was all new to me, and I was also very naïve. Although I was concerned, I knew that I was a law-abiding citizen who worked, paid taxes, and was a respectful person. Despite the abuse I had tolerated during my marriage, there was never any domestic violence. Not once did Diane or I call for the police, nor was there any violence between us, physical or otherwise. We certainly had arguments, but none that I remember the girls witnessed until the final month or two of our living together.

If you're keeping track of the many mistakes I made, don't miss this one: always use an attorney in court. I wish I had. I was remorseful and embarrassed, as well as naïve as to the etiquette and protocols of the courtroom, and I decided to plead guilty. I didn't see the need to pay an attorney to do that. But I underestimated the absolute deference that most judges are expecting, and going into their court without an attorney (for issues beyond speeding tickets, etc.) is the first indication to a judge that you're not taking the situation seriously enough. Those who have never been in court as a defendant may not fully understand the inequities of our legal system. The reality is that whenever human beings are involved there will be inconsistencies, personal biases, and mistakes. It's particularly bothersome to me that two materially similar cases can receive radically different results depending on the courtroom in which the cases are heard. Results can vary widely when cases are heard in different states, counties, or even with different judges in the same courthouse. As I was to learn, some areas of the country have judges who feel it's their duty to be as hard-assed as they possibly can. Who isn't supportive of being tough on crime? It's therefore easy to justify the behavior of such judges. Given that judges are human beings, however, those who are committed to being hard-asses are more likely to make bigger mistakes since they are also punishing some non-guilty people more harshly (if you believe only guilty people get punished you're as naive as I was). Or there may be extenuating circumstances that a judge will ignore because playing the role of a hard-ass has become his or her *modus operandi*. It's a scary reality. I can't say I know of a better alternative, but the idea that we give human beings the right to rule so conclusively over others who they may not like for any number of reasons is increasingly frightening to me. Unfortunately, it was nothing I paid attention to before my own experience in court. (I'm fully aware of the appeal process inherent in our legal system, but ask someone who went to jail because his ex-spouse falsely accused him of something if an appeal is even an option. Courtroom depictions on television falsely alter the perceptions of many regarding the realities of the legal process.)

Unfortunately, the area of central Pennsylvania in which we lived has a county courthouse that is generally considered one of the toughest in the state. This is partly due to the generally conservative, religious nature of the area. (I will not address the hypocrisy of an area that is geographically religious, and therefore theoretically tolerant, electing conservative judges who believe they're empowered directly by God to sentence others as strictly as possible.)

Let me now turn my attention to attorneys. As noted, I chose to streamline our separation agreement (thereby lessening expenses) by minimizing my use of an attorney. Diane took full advantage of one of the better-known law firms in the county. To be fair, she made her choice and I made mine. No one was forced to act one way or the other, but I was appalled at the intensity with which her attorney pushed the limits of professional ethics. I have been in the business world for many years and have participated in many contract negotiations (and even drafted a few contracts myself). Diane's attorney inserted clauses that were ethically questionable in terms of legality. There was absolutely no regard for what was reasonable or that which constituted a fair compromise. Bullying tactics and threats within the context of court procedures and costs were a constant strategy. I remember thinking how the actions of Diane's attorney were adding significant venom and bad will into a process that was already fraught with emotional landmines. It's too bad that attorneys practicing divorce law are not trained in family sensitivities surrounding custody-related issues. Many extract a few extra dollars for their clients at the risk of further disrupting the emotional equilibrium of the family unit, which hurts everyone, especially the children.

When I went into court for the hearing on Diane's restraining order against me, I had no idea what to expect. Without an attorney, I simply waited to be called into courtroom. Once inside, and after the court protocol of stating the reason for the hearing was read, Diane requested a continuance since her legal counsel had a conflict. Continuances are fairly common at the initial hearing since it is normally scheduled with relatively short notice. The continuance was granted, and I was warned by the judge that I was to have only written contact with Diane and that I was not to harass her in any way. That was fine by me.

In the meantime Diane was still sending the girls over with bills for expenses that she should have been paying herself. I can't tell you how aggravating it was to have the girls hand me an envelope while telling me, "Mom said you need to pay this." I now understand that this was another manifestation of her narcissism, the expectation that she should be treated specially and continually catered to in every way. I finally decided to put a stop to it. After writing a check to Diane for a legitimate expense, I put the following note to her in the envelope with the check.

> Enclosed is a check for XXX, which is the part of the expense request you recently provided me that I am legally obligated to pay as per our separation agreement. I will also pay, for the last time, the expenses related to repairs of the Mercedes, and the cell phone expenses. These expenses will be paid to you in the next couple of weeks.
>
> As you know, I have met all the financial obligations imposed on me by our agreement, which I will continue to do. As you know, I have been paying expenses I am not obligated to pay. I will no longer continue to do so.
>
> You have primary custody of the girls, and I pay you monthly support for them, among other expenses. It's clear you were irresponsible in your decision to purchase a townhouse beyond your ability to afford financially. Hence, you have been falsely communicating to me that I have obligations to pay for expenses which are not addressed at all in our agreement.

You were provided with 65% of our marital assets upon our separation and you have, in my opinion, an obligation to utilize those assets for the welfare of the girls.

Also, you refused my request to file jointly for the last tax year, and therefore cost me several thousands of dollars in unnecessary tax payments. You refused my offer to provide you with $2,400 for your agreement to file jointly. This money could have been used by you for the welfare of the girls. Obviously you didn't feel that was a worthwhile effort/decision for you to make.

You clearly have enough money to continue to party/socialize with your friends. I think you should focus your resources on the welfare of the girls instead.

Please continue to enjoy your role as primary custodian of the girls, but please also understand that the decisions you've made regarding our separation and your living arrangements are your responsibility. I am not obligated to pay for expenses beyond what are required by the agreement.

I felt this note was long overdue. It certainly wasn't my intention to unduly criticize her, but I felt it was necessary to clarify these important issues, especially given that she had benefited from my extra expense payments while violating my custody at the same time.

When I went back to court for the rescheduled hearing (again with no attorney), the county assistant prosecutor requested that I be given a two-year restraining order that would restrict me to email correspondence with Diane that was related specifically to the girls. I would also need to maintain a reasonable physical distance from Diane as much as possible. I would be allowed to attend all of the girls' activities whether Diane was there or not. I asked the judge a few questions in order to try and understand what constituted acceptable email subjects. I certainly did not want to violate the order in any way. The judge became visibly agitated at my questions and made a comment to the effect that he wasn't sure what the motivation was for my questions. It was clear he wasn't interested in directly communicating with the "accused," and since I didn't have an attorney, he was very dismissive. I presented no objection to the restraining order as requested, and it was therefore ordered by the judge.

As I stood up to leave the courtroom, one of the constables told me to wait a moment. The next thing I knew, he was pulling my hands behind my back and placing handcuffs on me. Unbelievably, Diane had called the police when she received my note with the check and said she found it to be harassing. Even more unbelievable was the fact that the police officer agreed. And incredibly, the county assistant prosecutor agreed that the note was harassing and agreed to press charges against me for a restraining order violation. I truly couldn't believe it. Where was rational thinking in this situation? Was this a joke? The woman for whom I had provided a comfortable stay-at-home lifestyle for seventeen years, and with whom I had created and shared the lives of two daughters, had just had me arrested for telling her I wouldn't pay any extra expenses going forward.

It was at that moment that I truly realized just how sick Diane was. Once I told her that there were no extra dollars coming her way, she lost all use for me in true narcissistic fashion. And worse yet, she sat my girls down and told them about my arrest, implying that I was a very bad person. The giddiness she must have felt to know the level of control she had just exerted over me must have been euphoric for her.

One thing I've learned from Diane is that, as with many narcissists, there is rarely any compromise. Everything is essentially a zero-sum game. If they don't win, they feel like they've lost. Nothing in-between is possible. A significant reason for this attitude is that narcissists have no ability to empathize. They know what they feel and don't care about the feelings of others. To acknowledge the feelings of others is to display empathy, but having empathy would sabotage their desire to win at any cost. Acknowledging the feelings of others is simply out of the question. Marrying a narcissist is a sure way to never have your own needs met.

I was now enveloped in a kangaroo county court system. I never expected any special treatment. When I screw up, I admit it and take the consequences. But I truly could not believe I had been arrested. As if to confirm my exasperation, two police officers, separately, stopped at my house over the next couple of weeks to apologize to me and basically say the same thing: they didn't become police officers to arrest people for the type of offense I had supposedly committed. They warned me that the assistant prosecutor was notorious for prosecuting alleged crimes like this one. They had seen firsthand how easily women are granted restraining orders, only to use the order as a means of harassment. This was about to happen to me, too. I never thought things could get as bad as they were about to.

A short while later I was approached by a friend who worked with a woman who had dated Dave immediately prior to his dating Diane. My friend said that Dave had dated her friend, Belinda, for several months and had gotten serious with her fairly quickly. According to my friend, Dave had told Belinda that he was in love with her and hoped that Belinda would help him decorate his house. She then continued to say that Dave had suddenly broken off the relationship with Belinda with no explanation, which hurt Belinda significantly. My friend realized that the reason for Dave's unceremonious dumping of Belinda was because he'd met Diane. This certainly wasn't any of my business beyond the fact that my girls would be hurt if Dave followed the same pattern with Diane.

A couple of weeks later I sent two emails to Diane in hopes of trying to make things better for all of us. The first message said:

"I confirmed with Brooke that I will pick her up @ 5:00 – they will leave no later than 8:00. I think it's best for the girls that I have a better relationship with Dave – please tell him to call/text me to get together for a beer. Thanks."

The second message said:

"I'm a bit concerned for the girls because I believe they (and you) are being played by a con man (Dave). Thanks."

I know referring to Dave as a con man wasn't the smartest thing to do, but I had legitimate concerns about how well Diane even knew him given how quickly she had brought him into our girls' lives. And I truly thought it was wise to get on friendly terms with him so there would be less tension between us, which would make the girls feel more comfortable. Looking back, I can't believe how naïve I was after having been arrested by Diane.

It's important to note here that the restraining order allowed me to send Diane emails which were 'civil in nature, and in reference to the girls'. I never considered that those two emails were anything other than civil and in reference to the girls.

A week later, as I was leaving a business function, my cell phone rang. A township constable was on the line, informing me that he had an arrest warrant for me. I actually chuckled since it didn't even register with me that there was any possibility that this could be the case. But I quickly realized he wasn't joking. Diane had once again called the police, claiming that the two emails I had sent referencing Dave were a violation of the restraining order. And once again, the same police officer had agreed that it was an infraction worthy of taking to the prosecutor's office. Throughout my entire experience of legal abuse by Diane, she continually called the same police officer, who always escorted Diane to and from court, as if he had appointed himself her personal bodyguard. I thought it interesting that I'd had two other police officers from the same township come to my house and apologize for what they said amounted to harassment of me by Diane, and yet this other officer had a significantly different attitude. When I subsequently asked one of the officers who visited my house if he would have taken those emails to the prosecutor, he said he would have told Diane that neither email justified the claim of a violation of the restraining order since I was allowed email contact with her. I became even more jaded about the specious way in which our legal system is implemented. It definitely helps to have friends in law enforcement, and Diane, it seemed, had made a useful friend.

This time I was at least smart enough to get an attorney. I assumed that, once the judge saw the two emails, he would almost feel the need to suppress his indignation at having his valuable time, and public resources, wasted on such an obviously trivial and misguided charge. I thought it might even teach Diane a lesson about bringing frivolous charges against me. I truly thought that I'd get the satisfaction of seeing her dressed down in court by the judge. In short, I wasn't too worried.

But I was angry. Attorney fees weren't cheap—several thousands of dollars, in fact—exactly the type of expense I had tried to avoid from the outset. Diane, on the other hand, had no legal expenses since she was using a free county resource designed to help women who were victims of domestic violence defend themselves. Yes, Diane was now legally considered a victim of domestic violence. She portrayed herself as a harassed ex-wife who was being relentlessly abused by her ex-husband. I felt that I had landed in an alternate universe in which everything was the opposite of natural reality. Even the counselor I was seeing on a regular basis couldn't believe what was happening to me. In fact, she felt a bit guilty since it had been she who'd suggested I reach out by email to Diane in order to have a beer with Dave for the girls' sake.

Diane again made sure to tell my daughters that I had been arrested. In what seemed to me the most diabolical effort on her part thus far, she told my girls that if she hadn't called the police both times that she herself would get in trouble with law enforcement. I heard this directly from Laurie, who had parroted it to me as a means of defending Diane's behavior. I was floored. I had hoped that my daughters, especially Laurie, would ask Diane why she would call the police on their dad, and for what reason. For seventeen years I was a great dad to both of them. How could they believe that the person they knew me to be for so long had suddenly become someone who deserved to be arrested, not just once, but twice? It was truly heartbreaking. It never occurred to me that my girls could be so easily manipulated by Diane's lies. I was just beginning to understand a lot of things, and I had no idea how much worse things would get or just how effective parental alienation can be.

Still, though, I figured my most recent arrest was a minor issue which, although expensive, wouldn't amount to much. Then I started having conversations with my attorney. Unfortunately, I was going to be in front of the same judge who had been so abrasive when I was in court the first time. I didn't realize at the time just how strong his reputation was for being an absolute hard-ass. My attorney actually described him as "crazy." The worst part was that I could see that my attorney was truly scared of this judge. He was palpably frightened, which started to make me think I should be concerned as well. Instead, I focused on calming my attorney down. What I didn't fully appreciate was that he had seen some crazy things in this courtroom, and particularly from this judge. What I didn't know at the time was that this judge was the former District Attorney in this same county, and courthouse (I've since developed the opinion that judges shouldn't be appointed in the same county in which they have worked in another capacity….the established relationships with colleagues, and potential long-standing allegiances, are much too ingrained many times to expect the required objectivity.)

My attorney also knew that there would be no sweet deals from the assistant prosecutor, who he described as a pit bull. That description wasn't hard for me to believe because it was this same prosecutor who had made the final decision on whether to proceed with legal action based on the evidence. This was the second time that she had looked at the messages I had written to Diane and decided to take me to court. It all seemed beyond bizarre to me. Did no one care that I was paying very substantial financial support for Diane and the girls and had made every payment in full and on time? Was no one willing to ask themselves if these frivolous charges against me were not a possible indication that Diane had control issues and possibly a mental disorder? Didn't my squeaky clean criminal record for forty-nine years (and unassailable marital behavior for seventeen years) count for anything? How about the fact that I was a great father who provided a financially and emotionally stable home environment for my girls? Had I done anything threatening, violent, or harassing?

I was beginning to truly hate a legal system that could be so easily manipulated by seemingly anyone for destructive and evil purposes. This legal system seemed to have even less of a social conscience than Diane herself. The thought that Diane was enjoying harassing me and telling the girls what was happening to me, and that having me arrested was the only choice she had, was hard to tolerate. I had long ago realized that I likely had never truly been in love with Diane, but I was certain now that I despised her.

On the day of the court hearing, my attorney was adamant that I not say anything unless directed to by the judge. That was fine by me since I was paying him to represent me better than I could represent myself. He had warned me repeatedly that I could be sentenced to as much as six months in prison. I was honestly incredulous at this suggestion and kept asking him if he remembered the two emails I had written. I honestly couldn't believe I was facing the threat of prison time. If anyone deserved to go to prison, I felt it should be Diane. Did anyone care how I would continue to pay child support, alimony, and all the other expenses while in prison? I could see that my attorney thought prison was a realistic option. What seemed even crazier to me was that a restraining order in Pennsylvania is a civil matter, not a criminal issue. Having a restraining order against me didn't mean I had a criminal record. It was a court-ordered action based on a civil complaint. How the hell could I go to prison for those two emails? Something seemed very wrong with the way the system worked. I wondered how many other people have been abused by nefarious ex-spouses, facilitated by a significantly dysfunctional legal system?

Prior to entering the court room, my attorney met with the assistant prosecutor and relayed to me an offer that was being proposed. I could accept six months probation and attend a domestic violence program for twenty-six weeks, two hours per week. I immediately said no. The idea that I would be considered a domestic violence offender was abhorrent to me, and accepting probation was creating a criminal record for myself. Why would I accept such terms based on what I considered bullshit circumstances? Wasn't there a chance that the judge would see this situation for what is was, a frivolous, non-violent charge? My attorney was adamant. He kept telling me I might go to prison. He said he'd seen it happen too many times with this judge. I relented, but I wasn't happy about it.

When we went into court, the judge asked me if I understood the issues involved and the offer that had been made, and I responded that I did. He asked me if I understood that I had no obligation to accept a plea and if I was sure I wasn't being coerced in any way. He also reminded me that I could otherwise get up to six months in prison. I honestly felt I wanted to make a stand and call the judge's bluff regarding prison. I requested that I be able to speak to my attorney in private, and we were instructed to walk out of the courtroom to confer with each other. Once out in the hall, my attorney looked like he might have a heart attack. He kept walking in a circle around me, repeating over and over, "You're going to prison, and I hope you understand that." Seeing him that distraught made me realize that tempting fate was worse than accepting probation. We walked back into court, and I accepted the plea.

I was now required to see a probation officer every two weeks and attended the domestic violence program every Thursday morning from eight until ten. I was the only one in the class that hadn't committed a violent act. Listening to the other attendees' stories of punching, slashing, smashing, and shooting their significant others made me nauseous. When it came time for me to explain why I was in the program, you can imagine the reaction from the others to my story of the two emails. Everyone thought I was lying at first until one of the facilitators actually read my arrest report as proof.

The thought that I had actually been married to the woman who put me here was even more nauseous than the stories I was hearing from this group. It made me think back to Diane's story of her nickname as a child: *comandante*. She was now in control, and what I didn't know or consider at the time was how ruthlessly she and Dave would use that control to harass and abuse me even more.

Chapter 7

Hurtful Betrayal

It was a continuing challenge to have a good relationship with my girls. Dave was becoming an increasingly serious presence in their lives, and they seemed to continue to withdraw from me as a result. I'm sure Diane felt everything was working as planned. She had the girls essentially full-time, my financial support, a new man, and the ability to harass me with the complicity of the law. I doubt she'd ever been happier.

It's also important to note that at this point I was not receiving any information from Diane or the girls concerning any of their school functions, dance recitals, talent shows, swim meets, etc. In fact, there were instances when Brooke had actually lied to me about whether she would be attending a swim meet or not in order to inhibit me from attending. And certainly Laurie was not providing me any useful information either. The message was increasingly clear, I was not considered an important part of the girls lives at this point. But kids don't normally behave this way without some prodding and encouragement from a parent. In fact, it's a well-accepted principle of post-divorce behavior that the parents are to keep each other informed of activities which involve the child(ren). To this day I still don't receive any communication regarding any of the girl's activities, from Diane or the girls.

One particular source of happiness for me was the increasing focus on Laurie's college plans. She had always been a good student, and attending college was something she was very much looking forward to. I took a certain amount of pride that I had made the financial resources available so that her college choice wasn't restricted by cost. Being her only parent to have attended college, I felt a particular qualification to take the lead in helping her make her choices. She had started to make a list of colleges she'd like to visit, and I was glad to help her make a visitation schedule. I remember how fun it was to call the colleges myself to proudly ask when prospective freshman could visit and to learn the visitation events schedule.

Laurie eventually made a list of five colleges located throughout the states of Pennsylvania, Delaware, Virginia, and West Virginia. Over the course of a couple of months, she and I visited all five campuses and I remember how proud I felt to have a daughter so eager and prepared to enter adulthood. I was also proud of her college choices and looked forward to becoming the parent of a college student.

Then came a betrayal I never saw coming and truly wasn't prepared for. It started one evening when Laurie called me to say she was filling out a couple of college applications and needed me to provide forty dollars for each of the application fees. She asked me for my credit card number to put on the applications. I immediately became uneasy. Because she lived full-time with Diane, I wasn't inclined to provide my credit card so that Diane might have access to it. I was still fuming about the two times Diane had me arrested, and I now understood that I had no idea what she was ultimately capable of. I told Laurie politely that I would provide a check for the application fees or reimburse her mother if she wanted to use her credit card. Laurie didn't like these choices and hung up in a bit of a huff.

The next day I received an email from Laurie that both broke my heart and shattered the hopes I had that she and I would be able to navigate this increasingly poisonous situation. In her email Laurie justified my arrests by Diane by stating that I "knew the terms and therefore deserved the consequences." She went on to say that she knew I was "legally binded [*sic*] to pay at least part of the many expenses and that I should want to help her and Brooke because they were my children". I was crushed. I honestly couldn't breathe. I didn't see this coming and wasn't emotionally prepared for it. Especially not after all I'd recently been through. It honestly felt like Laurie was acting like Diane towards me. I simply couldn't accept what were clearly inappropriate comments from a daughter to a father. I understand teenagers develop attitudes towards their parents, but this was different. I simply wasn't emotionally capable of dealing with this feedback given that I had been abused psychologically by Diane for so long and also traumatized by the arrests. Given that Laurie was spending virtually all of her time with Diane and Dave, I knew there was more to this feedback from her than typical teenage backtalk. It especially stung given the effort I'd recently made to take her on the college visits.

I needed to avoid any more pain and abuse. I'd like to say that I was strong enough to react in an admirably mature fashion and somehow just ignore the comments, but that wasn't the case. It didn't help that my counselor was even more appalled than I was. She had adopted a very protective attitude towards me that I truly appreciated. She couldn't believe I had been arrested twice either, and she seemed to despise Diane almost as much as I did. Being a mother herself, she was downright outraged that *any* mother would behave the way Diane was.

Laurie's comments served to create a wedge between her and me. I honestly couldn't open up myself to more hurtful lectures at that point. What particularly hurt was that it wasn't that long ago that Laurie and I would frequently take walks around the neighborhood, discussing school, college, horses, her boyfriend, and many other things. It was great father-daughter time together, and I enjoyed every minute of it. Several times neighbors commented to me on how endearing they found the sight of Laurie and I walking together. A couple of dads said they couldn't get their teenage daughters to speak to them regularly let alone take regular walks together. It was another source of pride for me.

It was extremely hard for me to spend so much time alone while my daughters were spending all their quality time with Diane and Dave. People who haven't gone through a divorce can't truly understand the reality of being replaced by another influence. Diane has never once had to experience the reality of another woman's influence on the girls while they were with me. Given her nature as a control-freak, I doubt she'd ever be able to tolerate it. That's partially why she made sure to bring Dave into the girls' lives as quickly as she did. She needed to take control and create a surrogate family environment in order for the girls to feel comfortable away from me.

My sense of isolation, outrage, and betrayal was overwhelming. I was now convinced that I was fighting against a strong tide of aggressive alienation by Diane. The hurtful comments from Laurie were significantly out of character for her and sounded as if they had come directly from Diane herself. Deep down I knew the girls were being brainwashed by Diane, but the pain and disappointment from such a hurtful betrayal from a daughter I loved so much and had spent so much time with over the years was another dagger in my heart at a time when I was already emotionally reeling. I didn't see any way to combat what I felt were significant forces against me.

I was particularly concerned about my relationship with Brooke since she was so much younger, and I knew she was even more capable of being influenced by misinformation and parental alienation. What kept me hopeful all along, I realized, was that Laurie and I had a longer history and had shared more experiences as father and daughter. It never occurred to me, especially after the time we spent together visiting colleges, that anything could crack the bonds between us. Looking back, one of the things that bothered me the most was what it took to crack those bonds—a total of eighty dollars for college applications. I simply had preferred to provide a check instead of my credit card for obvious reasons. Maybe my bonds with her weren't as strong as I had thought. That thought scared and saddened me deeply.

It turns out that there were several more hurtful experiences to come with Laurie. I deserve part of the blame because I was now angry and untrusting of almost everything that involved the girls. It seemed to me that every aspect of my relationship with them was being controlled by Diane, and possibly Dave.

I still enjoyed seeing Brooke. She had decided to join the school basketball team, and we spent hours playing basketball together in my driveway. Having been very athletic myself in high school and college, it was fun for me to watch her develop her skill and interest in sports. That spring she decided to play softball as well. We went out together to a sporting goods store and purchased the necessary equipment: bat, glove, and helmet. We spent hours outside my house playing catch or with me pitching her batting practice. I was proud of her efforts and dedication. I was also happily surprised when she expressed an interest in pitching as well. Pitching in softball requires an underhand technique that isn't necessarily a natural motion for most people. It also makes you the focus of most of the activity during the game. It was great for me to see Brooke show the level of confidence and commitment it took to learn to pitch and to take that level of responsibility during the games. I helped her as much as I could and enjoyed it as much as she did.

An event took place around this time involving both Laurie and Brooke that will always stand out for me as one of the highlights of being their father, and a great source of pride. Laurie's high school was presenting *The Sound of Music* that year, and both Laurie and Brooke were interested in trying out for the play. It was Laurie's junior year, and Brooke was in fifth grade. Laurie had taken voice lessons for many years and has a very special voice. She had been selected to participate in her high school's Concert Choir since her sophomore year. She was also now selected to play one if the nuns in the play and was awarded the opening solo. It was a special honor for a special girl.

The play required a couple of grammar school kids to play the children's roles, and kids from several schools in the area were notified about the opportunity. Since the roles involved singing skills as well as acting competence, the process turned out to be quite selective. I still remember the moment that Brooke received the phone call that she had been chosen to be in the play and would be playing the role of Brigitta. The pride I felt at having both my girls performing together is indelibly imprinted forever on my heart and soul.

I naturally went to all four performances of the play, and was enraptured each time as I watched my girls and enjoyed the quality of all the performers. Laurie performed her solo each time with perfect angelic pitch. Watching Brooke bring Brigitta to life with her special inflections, facial expressions, and wonderful singing was a bit overwhelming. I'll admit I was emotional with pride each time. Never could a father be more proud of his girls.

But things otherwise continued to be a challenge. Shortly after Thanksgiving that same year, I asked Brooke what she'd like as an upcoming Christmas gift. She had a cell phone by this time, which was very useful for the two of us to keep in touch. Her phone was an old hand-me-down model that had several performance issues. She indicated that her biggest wish that year was to upgrade her phone. I thought that was a good idea and told her we would pick out a suitable phone before Christmas. When we went to look at phones, I told Brooke that I wanted to make an agreement with her. I would buy her the phone if we agreed to text each other every morning to say "I love you" because I missed daily contact with her. Texting at least once a day would make me feel more connected to her. She eagerly agreed. For the next two months we texted as agreed every morning, and I looked forward to that special bit of contact as a start to my day.

Shortly thereafter I noticed that she didn't have the phone I'd purchased at Christmas and asked her what happened to it. Unbelievably, she told me that earlier that week Diane had taken the phone from her and told her that she was giving it to an attorney. I couldn't believe what I had heard. I asked her to repeat herself. It was true. Diane had confiscated my Christmas gift to my daughter and, even worse, had told our eleven year old that it was now in the hands of an attorney. I asked Brooke why her mom had given it to an attorney, and she said she had no idea.

This act by Diane was so diabolically cruel and inappropriate to both Brooke and me that I couldn't sleep for several nights. My counselor described this act by Diane as "controllingly wicked." I immediately sent an email to Diane's attorney requesting an explanation and to ask if she had Brooke's phone. I never received a response from the attorney, but when I subsequently asked the attorney directly during a meeting with her and Diane, she denied having the phone. I never got any explanation as to where the phone went or why it had disappeared, and Brooke never got the phone back. I am absolutely convinced Diane never had any intention of giving the phone to an attorney, and only confiscated it as another (successful) parental alienation effort.

The abuse continued to take its toll on me. I couldn't help but think about how much of an evil genius Diane was. Her taking the phone put a wedge between Brooke and me since the implication was that I had done something so wrong that it necessitated an attorney to become involved with her phone. Diane obviously felt increasingly empowered to act in any way she wanted. I couldn't help but notice that her inappropriate behavior increased as her relationship with Dave continued to develop.

With the restraining order against me firmly in place for two years, she started to use it as a way to keep me away from Brooke. One example involved a basketball function in which Brooke's team was making posters for their opening game. The posters were to be hung on the gym walls prior to the game, the sort of activity that eleven and twelve-year-old girls thoroughly enjoy. A message was sent out for parent volunteers to help facilitate and support the girls' efforts. Having spent so much time practicing basketball with Brooke, I felt a particular connection to her basketball efforts and her team and made plans to attend the function. I had no restrictions regarding attending such activities regardless of whether Diane was there or not. I simply needed to stay away from any purposeful interaction with her as spelled out in the restraining order. But I knew better than to trust Diane, so I purposely put a copy of the restraining order in my car.

When I arrived at the school gym to help with the posters, I greeted Brooke and her friends who were enthusiastically immersed in using paint, brushes, and poster board. I said hello to the coach and the other parents and planned to comfortably enjoy the excitement and energy only eleven and twelve-year-old girls can generate. Diane, however, had other ideas. Not long after I arrived, she came into the gym from the parking lot. As soon as she saw me, she whirled around dramatically and walked out the doors into the glass foyer of the gym. She pulled out her cell phone and made a very intentional effort to stare at me as she dialed the phone. It was clear she wanted me to believe she was calling the police. My heart sank. Was I ever going to be able to enjoy time with Brooke without Diane's sick and diabolical efforts to control me? I knew that I needed to get the restraining order from the car and, with more than a little embarrassment, take the coach aside to make him aware of the situation and ask him to be a witness that I had not had any interaction with Diane. As I walked past Diane to the parking lot, I distinctly heard her saying my name and spelling it out.

I got the paperwork from the car, went back in, and asked the coach to step aside with me. I showed him the language in the order that made it clear I was perfectly entitled to be there. I knew I couldn't have the girls on the team witness the police come to the gym even though I was doing nothing wrong. It would certainly cause Brooke stress and embarrassment and put a serious damper on the entire event for all the girls. So I left, privately fuming. Diane had won yet again.

At one of our subsequent court appearances, I told the judge about this incident and how the restraining order against me was being used by Diane to harass and control me. The judge looked at the assistant prosecutor and asked her to confer with Diane about the claim I had just made. After their conference, the assistant prosecutor stated emphatically that Diane insisted she had not been on the phone with the police and went further by stating that it seemed I had been inappropriately eavesdropping on Diane's conversation. I still remember the judge looking at me and telling me how 'presumptuous' it was of me to assume that Diane was calling the police. Although I was damn sure I knew that she had wanted me to believe she was calling the police in order to get me to leave, I didn't have any proof.

About a week later I drove to the township police department to get some advice as to how to handle future efforts by Diane to control me. As I drove into the parking lot, an officer was walking into the building. I rolled down my window and asked him if I could talk with him for a second. I explained that I had an existing restraining order against me and was looking for some advice. He was very friendly and invited me into his office. When I told him my name and started to explain the story to him, he stopped me and asked if my ex's name was Diane. I said it was, and he proceeded to tell me that she had indeed called the police the evening of the basketball event and that he was the one who took the phone call from her. He recounted how she requested that an officer be dispatched to the gymnasium to remove me from the premises. He said he went into station files and pulled out a copy of the restraining order, which clearly stated I had the right to attend any of my daughter's activities. He said he told Diane that there was no cause for him to go to the gym and remove me. But by that time, Diane had already achieved her objective.

This incident was appalling on several levels. The blatant effort by Diane to harass me and have me leave the gym was bad enough. But to deprive my daughter of my support and interaction was even worse. She had blatantly lied to a judge by denying she had called the police. I couldn't believe how backward everything seemed. Diane was the one acting inappropriately and illegally, and yet she was the one with the support of the law to control and harass me. And all the while I was still dutifully paying her my required financial support that, maddeningly, served to make her life as comfortable as possible while she tortured me.

Chapter 8

Prison

I was thankful to have the continuing support of my counselor. I was nevertheless sinking into an emotional malaise from which there seemed no escape. Parents are tethered to their kids by special heart strings. It's unnatural to suddenly find yourself isolated from the children you've raised from birth and spent so much time with. It's hard enough for most parents to watch their kids leave for college. In that case, however, there has at least been a progression from childhood to legal adulthood which, although it passes all too quickly, completes the typical phases of parental involvement most parents experience. In my case, I went from being a fully engaged dad to my ten-year-old daughter to being replaced by another man's presence and being purposely alienated from her. There was no transition period for either of us. I was left with financial obligations but no daughter. There was nothing inadvertent or accidental about it. It was a conscious, malicious, and diabolical effort that was being successfully implemented.

It was all a very effective form of psychological abuse. In the same way Diane had been abusive to me during our marriage, she was now using all resources available to her in every possible way: the law, Dave, and the naiveté and vulnerability of the girls. It was very hard to tolerate, even more so than I can explain in words. I kept thinking that it shouldn't be this easy for her. Where was the true justice in this situation? But I wasn't emotionally able to see at that point that I was imposing rational expectations on an irrational person.

Worst of all, the girls were being told that I was a bad person, someone who'd been arrested twice (thus far). I can only speculate that, from the girls' perspective, they assumed that the police were the best judges of what constitutes appropriate behavior. Children would have no reason to believe otherwise, especially when they are being told this by their mother. It was hard for me to accept that the many years of my efforts as their dad seemed to count for very little in their minds. It's easy for me now to see just how vulnerable they both were to Diane's manipulation and disinformation. They, too, were victims of the entire divorce experience and Diane's malicious behavior. Unfortunately, I was in no position to be rational at the time given the abuse I was being subjected to.

My counselor told me that she had never seen a more vicious effort by a mom to alienate and control the children. Several times we discussed how to reach out to the kids in ways that wouldn't end up making things worse for them, and me. The fact that I had incurred a legal violation of Diane's restraining order gave her all the leverage she needed. Being on probation makes everyone's perception of you different. You're now someone who has been judged guilty by a court of law. How could there be any mistake about that?

Finally, my counselor and I agreed that I needed to get a legal custody order to make sure I had as much leverage as possible in protecting my right to see Brooke. I had avoided this since my probation could certainly be exploited by Diane and her attorney to minimize my allotted time with her. Furthermore, I would undoubtedly be characterized as a danger in some way. Understandably, the courts tend to take these issues seriously. I wasn't sure I was in the necessary emotional state to have Diane use her lies in court to yet again abuse and mischaracterize me, but we felt we had no choice.

My attorney sent a letter to Diane's attorney stating that I intended to pursue a court-ordered custody arrangement. My attorney suggested that we offer a reasonable and relatively standard visitation schedule that could be agreed to and subsequently filed with the court. This would enable us to avoid further contentiousness by eliminating the need for any more court involvement than was necessary. Hopefully, it would eliminate any possibility that my daughters would need to appear in court. We sent the letter and waited for a response, which never came.

In the meantime, I continued to see Brooke for a few hours each Sunday afternoon whenever there was no excuse made that she wouldn't be available. I still looked forward to seeing her very much, and we spent many hours together at Barnes and Noble reading, talking, and enjoy snacks from the cafe.

One of the more hurtful post-divorce experiences for me took place around this time. As I got in my car to pick up Brooke at the appointed time one Sunday, I received a text from her asking if I could delay picking her up for another half hour. I texted her back, asking why. She replied by explaining that they were all at Laurie's high school play and were running a bit late. I couldn't believe what I had just read. No one had told me Laurie was involved in her high school play that year (it was her senior year) as she had been (along with Brooke) the previous year. Ever since her hurtful email to me a couple of months earlier, Laurie and I had had limited contact. I simply couldn't risk any more attitude from her.

I informed Brooke that I was already on my way over to get her and that I'd wait there until she arrived. I parked in the street as I always did in front of Diane's townhouse and waited. About five minutes later Dave's car came around the corner and parked in front of my car. Diane exited from the front passenger door and Brooke got out of the rear driver's side. Brooke walked immediately to my car and got in the front seat. Diane waved to Brooke and gave me a self-satisfied "we screwed you" smirk as she walked towards her townhouse. Her parents walked up to the sidewalk, and her father gave me a quick wave, which I returned. Diane walked into the townhouse as her father helped her mom up the front steps. Dave followed them inside. It took no more than forty-five seconds for all of them to enter the house. It was extremely hurtful to realize that they had all been at Laurie's school play, which I was purposely not informed about. I was emotionally crushed. How could they all continue to hurt me like this?

Frankly, I didn't think I could sink any lower emotionally after realizing just how resolute they all were in their efforts to keep me out of their lives. But it wasn't just Diane hurting me. Both girls knew I would have loved to see Laurie in her school play, but they had intentionally decided to not make me aware of her involvement. I had tasted this same rejection a couple of months earlier when I spontaneously attended a football game at Laurie's high school at the invitation of a neighbor. I was shocked to find out that Laurie was singing "The National Anthem" that night, which I was told nothing about. As I listened, I was proud but emotionally broken in so many ways.

A couple of weeks later I had just arrived home from errands on a Sunday evening at around eight o'clock. The weather was cool and crisp, and I decided to take a walk around the neighborhood, the same route Laurie and I had walked so many times together. As I started up the street, I noticed a police car parked against the curb. Passing the car, I waved hello and continued on. I then heard the car circle around behind me and stop. The officer called my name and instructed me to come over to the car. I was then able to see that it was Diane's policeman friend. The officer informed me that he had a warrant for my arrest and proceeded to put handcuffs on me and place me in the backseat of his car. I was shocked, confused, and increasingly pissed off. How could this be happening? I had done absolutely nothing to Diane or anyone else to deserve being arrested. And the fact that it was the same damn cop again made me start to consider the possibility that something inappropriate was taking place.

I repeatedly asked him to tell me why I was being arrested, but he ignored me in the arrogant and self-righteous manner that many cops exhibit (and that too many seem to enjoy). Once at the township station, I sat in the car outside the building for at least forty-five minutes while the officer talked on the radio and chatted with his colleagues. It almost seemed like he was purposely wasting time, but for what reason I had no idea. Finally, he told me that Diane and Dave had filed a police report claiming that an incident occurred when I'd picked up Brooke after Laurie's school play. It was now four weeks after that Sunday. He told me that they both claimed that I had parked my car in a manner as to block the front door and had glared angrily at Diane for a full three minutes before driving away from the townhouse with Brooke. I couldn't believe what I was hearing. This was total bullshit in every detail. I asked the cop how in the world I could have blocked the front door with my car since the driveway and garage are at the back of her property, not the front where I had parked. I related that my car had been parked in the street where I, and everyone including Diane, Laurie, and Dave, normally parked. He refused to answer any of my questions and it became clear that I was going to once again become the victim of a very sick ex-wife and a police officer who seemed to be conspiring with Diane.

I was eventually driven to the city police department, where I was fingerprinted. When I asked what the procedure was and if I was allowed to call someone, I was told that the judge had left about thirty minutes ago and therefore I would need to spend the night in a holding cell until he arrived again in the morning. It was hard not to feel like there was a master conspiracy against me, and my immediate thought was that it may not have been a coincidence that I sat in the police car for so long. Had the officer been waiting for the judge to go home? But that was the least of my worries. I was given a phone call, which I used to call a personal friend, Tom, who's an attorney. He doesn't practice criminal law, but I knew he would be able to contact my attorney's office in the morning to request that someone look at the circumstances of my arrest. I was then placed in a holding cell with nothing in it but a toilet and a metal bench. My head was spinning. My disgust for Diane hit an entirely new level, one I didn't think was possible. I lay there wondering how to deal with the contacts I wear in my eyes, which I normally took out each night but now had nowhere to store. I shivered in the unheated cell. With people yelling and doors constantly slamming, it dawned on me why my attorney and I had not received a reply from Diane regarding our custody letter. Diane and Dave had obviously come up with a better idea: have me arrested.

When morning finally arrived, everything seemed even more surreal than the night before. Some part of me naturally tried to ascribe my current situation to a dream......likely an involuntary reaction of my brain to circumstances it had no foundation to process. I was finally allowed to see the judge, which is when a sobering reality set in. Being arrested for another restraining order violation was bad enough, but I was currently on probation as well. This arrest was also a probation violation, a very serious matter. The judge set my bail at $20,000, but that was almost irrelevant. I didn't have the option of bail at this point. Due to the probation violation, I was going directly to prison until I had a hearing in front of the same damn hard-ass judge I'd seen previously. This wasn't good. For the first time I started getting nervous. Until then, I, like many falsely accused people, had just assumed that nothing horrendously bad could happen to me if I really hadn't done anything wrong. Being arrested, and getting probation, coupled with all the aggravation I had experienced from Diane's mental illness-fueled vendetta against me, seemed incredibly unjust, but I'd been able to handle it. But what would happen to my business if I was in prison? Could I actually keep my sanity while picturing Diane and Dave's glee at putting me behind bars. (I'm sure Dave's CIA friends were proud of him.) Even worse was knowing that Diane was probably already sitting down with my girls to tell them that their dad was in prison, and emphasizing how I couldn't behave properly no matter how much she and the police warned me. I'm sure she also again emphasized her previous bogus claim that she and Dave had no choice but to call the police given her legal responsibilities. Why would the girls believe anything different at this point? It was pure psycho-genius on Diane's part.

Later that morning, I was driven to the county prison. I started to wonder how I would be able to notify my business associates that I wouldn't be around for at least the next several days. And what would I tell them? I certainly wouldn't say that I was in prison. I hadn't shared the recent tribulations imposed on me by my psycho ex with anyone at this point—not any of the crazy details. I was now entering a whole new world, one I'd spent my life thinking was beyond any reality I'd ever experience. I prided myself on ethical and legal behavior. To this very day I've never even had a late payment on my credit report. I'm certainly far from perfect, but I do try to do the right thing. Being driven over to prison in handcuffs and shackles was humiliating, as was the strip search once I arrived. I was powerless. I honestly didn't deserve to be there, and there wasn't a damn thing I could do about it.

I was put in a cell on one of the strictest cell blocks in the prison…..even further indignation. I was allowed out of my cell only two hours each day, at which time I could try to use the phone (along with everyone else), take a walk in a circular area measuring approximately twenty feet in diameter (with twenty-foot high walls and an open roof area), watch television, or get to know my neighbors. Technically, I hadn't been sentenced to prison. I was simply being held there. Theoretically, when I got in front of the judge, he would see how stupid Diane and Dave's story was. I hoped he would wonder how I could have blocked the door by sitting in my car in the street, and that he'd understand that it could not have taken Diane three minutes to walk the twenty feet from the street to her front door. I hoped he would see that it was obviously bullshit. In fact, it was all so obviously false that even Diane's cop friend should have been held accountable for accepting such ridiculous claims. And certainly the assistant prosecutor should have given a skeptical eye to details that didn't make sense based on even cursory examination. But that's not how this county works. It doesn't abide by the law. The county *is* the law, and they are damn proud of it, too.

Prison is very disorienting, as I guess it's designed to be. No one cares that it's midnight and you'd rather sleep. No one cares that you don't prefer to be awakened at 5 a.m. for breakfast, but that's the way it works. No one cares that your psycho ex-wife and her boyfriend lied through their teeth to put you there. It's not their job to care; it's their job to make sure you never want to come back, assuming you ever get out. Frankly, I was surprised at the number of repeat offenders. Many of the inmates had relationships with each other that would make most siblings jealous. Their stories of different prisons in the area in which they'd spent time were actually pretty fascinating.

I can't tell you how many of the inmates, and even a couple of the COs (correctional officers), said to me "You don't look like you belong here." (Amen, brother). I remember thinking to myself that a person could not possibly have a conscience to subject the co-parent of your kids to these circumstances as a means of satisfying your dysfunctional need for control. I also remember thinking I would never again complain about airline food. Anyone who thinks they've had food that's inedible has never been in prison. I guess it's all part of the "We don't want you to want to be here" strategy. It's quite effective.

Amazingly, I was told (and it was true) that up until only a couple of months before I was locked up, the inmates on the cell block where I stayed were only allowed out of their cells for thirty minutes every twenty-four hours. They had recently changed that rule after two inmates jumped from the upper floor (where my cell was) and landed on their heads, killing themselves. This was no game. Locking people up is a form of torture. I'm not saying it isn't necessary, only that the legal system should make every attempt to be damn sure that people are guilty before applying such torture. In fact, I honestly think judges should spend a weekend in jail as a prerequisite to doing their jobs with the proper amount of sensitivity and empathy.

Making phone calls was basically impractical since anyone you call gets a message upon answering the phone that says the caller's name and that the call is coming from the county prison. There is then a series of instructions one needs to follow to create an account using a credit card so that he can speak with you. Yes, in order to receive a call from someone in that prison, one needs to pony up money, which is not a procedure conducive to calling casual acquaintances. Luckily, Tom became my savior in terms of making calls for me to business associates, telling them I'd had a death in the family (not mentioning it was my ego that had died) and taking care of some things at the house for me. He was a true friend when nothing less would have helped. I subsequently joked with him that he certainly knows I owe him the same favor if he's ever in prison.

I still had no idea how long I'd be there. I had no way of communicating with my attorney, but Tom spoke with him and relayed messages to me. I was told I could expect a visit from my attorney within a couple of days. I was still hopeful of getting out at any minute. What I hadn't been told yet was that I would not be getting out before my hearing with the judge. If that hearing didn't go well, I would likely be in prison for six months. I learned all this when my attorney was finally able to clear some time in his schedule to see me. Needless to say, that was a bit depressing.

I had a total of five "cellys" (cellmates, one at a time) while in prison. It was a fascinating experience to be locked up with perfect strangers. Everyone has a story, and there's lots of time to tell them. Luckily, I got along well with all of them. (I did, however, develop significant empathy for women who sleep with men who snore…brutal). Sleep is everyone's escape in prison. There are no walls in your dreams, and I spent nearly all my dream time with my girls. It kept me sane thinking and dreaming about them. But I also knew they were aware of where I was and that they would assume the worst about why I was there. That hurt and still does.

To pass the time, I took toilet paper and, using water and pressure, made layers of tissue into a ball. I spent hours throwing the ball off the cell wall at different angles to challenge myself to try and catch it. My cellys would join in the fun, too, and it helped pass the time. Luckily, I became friendly with one of the inmates who had been there long enough to have some special privileges and therefore had access to books. One day he slipped me two books while walking past my cell. I wasn't sure why he seemed so secretive about it, but I truly appreciated his help.

There's lots of mental illness in prison, and not all of it is a function of horrible prison conditions. One of my conclusions from my time in prison is that we, as a society, need a better way to diagnose and treat mental illness or we'll just keep building more prisons.

You can imagine the reactions I got from other inmates as to why I was in prison. Explaining that my ex and her boyfriend claimed I'd blocked the door to her home with my car and that I glared at her from the car just sounded ridiculous. They would say, "That's bullshit. You chased her with a bat, right?" Or "You beat the hell out of her boyfriend, right? It's okay. You can tell me. I've been there, too." The humiliation seemed to come from every angle.

I eventually received written notification that my hearing with the judge was scheduled in two days. I lay awake at night, hoping for the best. I also accepted the fact that, no matter what happened, I wouldn't let this experience break me. I purposely kept thinking that someday the girls would be out of Diane's control and that they would have a chance to see me again as the father and person they had always known—not the monster Diane was trying to get the girls to believe I was. I resolved not to give her the satisfaction of breaking me in any way that diminished my hope for the future. She might have been able to put me in prison, but she couldn't make me become as jaded as her.

On the day of my court hearing I was shuttled over to the county courthouse, again handcuffed and shackled. Knowing that I hadn't been convicted of any crime made me all the more aggravated, but I was at least hopeful that the judge would see how bizarre the details were and would believe me. I also couldn't stop thinking about how much pleasure Diane must have had each day knowing she'd put me in prison. I was sure that it must have been an almost euphoric rush for her sick and troubled mind. There's not much more control a control-freak can hope for.

I was put in a small cell with six or seven other men also awaiting their turn in court. It was natural for discussions to take place there concerning the details of one's alleged offenses. The details of my particular situation were a source of amusement for the others.

After several hours, my attorney came in and went over the details of what he would say to the judge and what I would likely be expected to contribute. It was all very serious, and it was at that point that I became nervous for the first time. If the judge decided against me, I could be shuttled directly back to prison for up to six months. I hadn't let that possibility weigh too heavily on my mind since it wouldn't have served a very useful purpose. I knew that letting myself be tortured by the thought of staying in prison would enable Diane to achieve her objective of continuing her psychological abuse. My attorney left and said he'd try to get an update as to when I would see the judge.

About ten minutes later my attorney entered the waiting cell again with a very disturbed look on his face. I asked him if something was wrong. He looked me in the eyes and told me that he had just seen Diane and Dave in the waiting area outside the courtroom and that they had Brooke with them. They planned to have her testify against me. A wave of nausea immediately rushed through my entire body. I honestly don't know how I didn't vomit. That moment will likely forever be the absolute worst moment of my life. I had endured significant psychological abuse, as my counselor and other professionals have all agreed, but I hadn't experienced anything close to the emotions of that moment.

The thought that Diane would bring Brooke into court to testify to the false police report she and Dave had filed against me was beyond appalling. The more I thought about it, the more it sickened me. Diane and Dave had to tell Brooke that she needed to skip school so that she could go into the court house and be called in front of the judge to say that I had done *what*—sit in the car with her for a full three minutes? That I had glared at her mother? Or did they want Brooke to add some additional details to make it sound even worse? The diabolical genius of it was as impressive as it was abhorrent. It was serving to alienate Brooke from me at a much deeper level by making her an active participant in the abusive charade. Diane's feeling of total control and omnipotence over me were going beyond any rational level. This is the point when I realized (and my counselor later agreed) that Diane had a sociopathic personality in addition to her narcissistic issues. There was no indication at this point that she was functioning with any type of normal conscience. Looking back, it seems obvious she'd had the same sociopathic issues for a long time.

I caught a break, however. I never went in front of the judge that day. My attorney said the schedule was backed up so that my hearing needed to be rescheduled. I was in such an emotional free-fall that I barely understood his explanation. I wondered if Brooke might have had an emotional reaction to the waiting and her impending court drama. She is a very sensitive girl, which sparked my outrage that Diane would even consider putting her through such a traumatic experience. But the fact that I avoided walking into the courtroom to see my eleven-year-old daughter testify against me was the luckiest break I had ever received. I don't think I could have recovered from that, especially if her testimony was a contributing factor to my getting sentenced to prison time. The guilt she would likely have felt as she grew older, knowing she'd been horribly manipulated by Diane, might well have been something Brooke would never have recovered from. (I've since learned that Diane told Brooke that she was required, subpoenaed, to go to court and therefore neither Diane nor Brooke had a choice in the matter.)

As previously mentioned, the female prosecutor (assistant District Attorney) had a reputation for being ruthless. Two township police officers told me that they didn't know any police officer in the county who wasn't intimidated by her. The charges against me were so trivial that the idea of prosecution seemed incredulous to everyone who's heard the details. But to think that my eleven-year-old daughter should be a party to the court proceedings was equally incredulous. Did anyone care what the short or long-term psychological effects might be on Brooke? Did her testimony really add much to the case, or was the case so ridiculous that the only sensible strategy was to use her as a witness?

I understand that administering any type of equitable national legal system is an onerous undertaking fraught with all the failings that human beings purposely or unwittingly muster. But when it comes to using the testimony of minor children in non-violent situations involving their parents, shouldn't the circumstances be deemed sufficiently compelling before their involvement is acceptable? Was my daughter going to verify that she knew I sat there for three full minutes? Young children have even less of a sense of accurate time passage than most adults. Surely the best Brooke could do was to confirm what Diane and Dave were already claiming.

We shouldn't leave the decision to bring a minor into the courtroom solely up to a prosecutor who likely has the sole motivation of maximizing the total number of convictions he or she can claim—someone who has no real interest, or training, in the subsequent emotional trauma that the child might endure. No one was claiming I did anything malicious to Brooke, then or ever. Children obviously need to be protected against every kind of abuse or exploitation by their parents or anyone else. In this situation, who was actually exploiting Brooke? The prosecutor wanted a conviction. Diane wanted to control and abuse me further while alienating Brooke even more. But what was in Brooke's best interest? Did anyone really care?

Maybe courts should adopt a procedure requiring a professional family counselor to make a judgment as to the necessity of bringing a minor into a courtroom to testify against a parent and whether a child might suffer emotional harm. Perhaps a written statement from the child could be presented in court without the need for the child to be traumatized by an actual physical appearance.

Lastly, is a mother who would voluntarily agree to bring a minor child into court to testify against a child's father regarding such bogus and trivial issues fit to be the majority custodian of that child? Should a prosecutor be able to subpoena a minor child for any reason, regardless of how trivial the issue?

Luckily for me and Brooke, the situation of facing each other in court didn't materialize. Luckier still, my attorney was able to convince the judge to authorize my release from prison until my rescheduled court appearance, which was seven days later. I had spent 10 days locked up.

I now had at least a week of freedom in front of me, although that week wasn't particularly enjoyable. I needed to deal with the real possibility of a six-month prison stay starting immediately after my upcoming court appearance. I assumed Brooke would be brought back to court to testify, which basically precluded me from getting much sleep that entire week. I went to see my counselor that week, and she literally cried.

As it turned out, I actually had two upcoming court appearances. The first one, which was the rescheduled appearance discussed above, was for my (second) alleged restraining order violation. For that offense alone, I could get up to six months in prison. Additionally, *any* criminal offense committed while on probation is considered a probation violation, which is a separate infraction from the actual offense itself. Restraining orders are a civil issue, not criminal, at least in Pennsylvania. A restraining order violation in Pennsylvania is a low-grade misdemeanor, below a grade-one misdemeanor, which is the lowest misdemeanor. While that was actually a good thing for my criminal history record because it didn't indicate a serious criminal past, it didn't mean that the judge wasn't entitled to put me in prison. I find this to be another area of the law with a serious disconnect between the offense and the punishment. Low-grade misdemeanors should be more limited as to how harsh a penalty which can be applied. If it's deemed reasonable to give someone six months in prison, then a restraining order should be considered a more serious offense than one that is lower than the lowest misdemeanor. Judges should be barred from treating such minor offenses as major violations of the law.

The day before my rescheduled hearing, my attorney got a call from the prosecutor's office offering a plea arrangement. The prosecutor was adamant at the time of my original hearing that there would be no plea offering for me, but my attorney tried several times to see if there were any options on the table. We were a bit surprised to find a last-minute offer. I had hoped that was because my daughter Brooke had balked at the emotional stress of enduring another courthouse visit. Or perhaps the prosecutor realized how ridiculous the evidence would sound in court. Regardless, the offer was that I would plead guilty to the charge of a restraining order violation and be given another six months probation instead of risking prison time. Additionally, the prosecutor's office would agree to recommend that I only get six months probation for the probation violation, for which I would have a separate hearing in a couple of weeks. I could have been given six months in prison for that offense as well, which meant that I was looking at the possibility of spending a year in prison. It's amazing how much damage a sociopathic, narcissistic ex-spouse can impose given the right circumstances and legal conspirators.

My attorney was very hesitant to recommend that I plead guilty to anything at all because of the trivial charges against me. He told me that he personally would like me to claim my innocence. But given that the judge was so unpredictable it would be a significant risk not to take the plea offer. (I subsequently spoke with a well-regarded attorney practicing in this same county who characterized this particular judge as 'corrupt'. This attorney had been a successful federal prosecutor previously, and I feel his opinion to be credible). My attorney insisted that I plead *nolo contendere*, which means "no contest" and carries no admission of guilt. Realistically though there's no practical distinction between a plea of *nolo contendere* and a guilty plea in terms of the judge's right to impose punishment.

I knew immediately, however, that I would take any plea deal offered since I would do anything to avoid making Brooke come into the courtroom. I'm not sure if I could have emotionally held it together should that have happened, and I simply couldn't imagine how I'd ever get the image of her in court out of my mind. I would have taken a year or more in prison to make sure she never had to deal with the emotional ramifications of having helped to punish her father for such bullshit charges. From my perspective, this was no time to for me to take a righteous stand. There was too much at stake for Brooke and me down the road. Things in that respect were already bad enough.

When I finally got into court it, was a very frustrating experience. To listen to the prosecutor recite the charges against me was just short of maddening. The prosecutor even added a detail of her own to make the charges sound even worse. What follows is the exact testimony taken from the court transcript.

Prosecutor: Your Honor, that incident occurred on XXXXXX at 1701 hours. It occurred at XXXXXXXXXXXXXXXXXXXX. There was to be a custody exchange between the parties and involving the parties' two daughters, specifically, their 11-year-old daughter. There was a musical at XXXXXXXXXX that the eldest daughter was in. It ran late, so the younger daughter sent a text message indicating that they would be a couple of minutes late for the exchange. When all the parties returned to the stated address, the defendant was waiting in his vehicle, the younger child exited her mother's vehicle (*my note: it was actually Dave's vehicle*), and went to her father's vehicle. The defendant then pulled his vehicle towards the end of the driveway directly in front of the residence. (*My note: there is no driveway in front of Diane's house; it's in the back of the house, which is where the garage is. And I never moved my vehicle other than when I drove away*)

My Attorney: Excuse me. Your Honor. May I have a moment?

Judge: All right

My Attorney: Okay.

Prosecutor: Your honor, the defendant did remain in front of the residence for a number of minutes. He did make eye contact with the plaintiff. He did glare at her in a manner that she found harassing and made her feel uncomfortable and uneasy. (*My note: this was truly unbelievable to listen to. I was facing possible prison time because of the claim I glared at my ex-wife, which made her uneasy(?). I was there for no more than 45 seconds...and, regardless,* *why would she stand there for 'a number of minutes' if she felt harassed and uneasy?)*

My Attorney: Forgive me, Your Honor. If I may, I had told the Assistant District Attorney, the gentleman that was handling the case last week had clarified and confirmed that my client was in a position where he should be waiting for them to arrive. He did not reposition his vehicle or move his vehicle in any manner. He was simply there longer than what some felt he needed to remain before leaving, which he ultimately did.

Judge: *Well, apparently there was a glare.* {italics added}

My Attorney: Arguably. But I wanted to clarify in terms of it wasn't a movement of the vehicle.

Judge: Prosecutor, do you agree that the defendant was entitled to be there for a custody exchange? Is that correct?

Prosecutor: That's correct, Your Honor

Judge: And you're acknowledging, sir, that you were there for the custody exchange?

Me: Yes, Your Honor

Judge: All right. Thank you.

My Attorney: I had spent a great deal of time meeting with my client and talking to him about the legal sufficiency of the Commonwealth's case in great detail, Your Honor. My partner and I have also sat down with him, and he is well aware of the case that he could put on should he decide to litigate this, and what the Commonwealth would have to prove.

After much discussion, it was my client's informed intent to resolve this matter because, in his mind, he cannot afford in any way, shape, or form to go back to prison given that he is the sole proprietor of his business. And rather than litigate this and take any risk of going back to prison—and he understands that there is a risk—he is willing to plead *nolo contendere* for the overall agreement that was represented to the court. We discussed in great detail the defense that we would have to put on, the legal standard of whether or not this arguably constitutes criminal conduct. But I am satisfied, as is my partner, that this plea is knowing, voluntary, and intelligent. He is well aware of all his options. And, frankly, the other consideration was last Wednesday he saw his young daughter outside the courtroom, I believe, waiting to testify as to how long he sat in the vehicle before he pulled away. He did not under any circumstances want to see his daughter here again under these circumstances. So all of these things played into his decision to enter his *nolo contendere* plea.

At any time the judge could have disallowed the plea deal and dismissed the charges due to the absurd nature of the entire case. But when I heard the judge say, "Well, apparently there was a glare," I knew I had made the right decision to take the deal. The judge was just waiting for the chance to find me guilty of something, anything. I ended up making it easy for him by agreeing to the plea deal, although it probably ruined his day to know I wasn't going back to prison.

The result of this court appearance, and the one that followed for the probation violation, was as follows.

- I received six months probation for each issue - the restraining order violation and the probation violation. The judge had the option of declaring that each six-month sentence run concurrently, but he chose consecutively, which meant I was on probation for another year.

- I was required to start my domestic violence meetings all over again, which meant that I ended up going weekly (for two hours), for a total of thirty weeks (including the ten weeks I had already completed before the new charges were brought against me).

This chaos all resulted because I sent two innocuous emails and because of the lies that Diane and Dave decided to tell. It was truly unbelievable.

Additionally I was told by the judge that if I appeared in his court again for any reason that probation wouldn't be an option. Translation: I was going to prison. He failed to mention, however, that I would need to be found guilty of something in order to be sentenced to prison. I guess the assumption of guilt was taken for granted.

It was another surreal occurrence in his kangaroo court. Sadly, it's the hard-ass efforts by judges (and others) which produce the unfair results that serve to encourage offenders (like Diane) to continue their destructive behavior.

Chapter 9

Losing the Girls

I continued to regularly see my counselor in order to make sense of what I was experiencing and to find meaningful ways at to cope. It wasn't easy. My counselor, being a mom herself, seemed almost as emotionally distraught about my circumstances as I was. Dealing with irrational people like Diane doesn't lend itself very easily to rational assessment and action plans. But my counselor kept me afloat at a time when sinking almost seemed preferable.

One of the issues we discussed was the fact that I was becoming increasingly irritated with my girls. It was harder than I can express to watch the girls become increasingly committed to Diane and Dave while simultaneously obviously disrespecting me. In retrospect, I wasn't capable of handling it well. Getting annoyed and angry is almost always a mistake, especially with kids, and especially in situations that kids don't have significant control over. And my getting annoyed was a mistake I would increasingly come to regret.

My situation was horrible in so many ways. I had no choice at this point but to communicate directly with my girls since any communication with Diane was legally forbidden. I was, for all intents and purposes, no longer their dad because I was communicating and negotiating with them on equal footing. I couldn't tell them to do anything because Diane was telling them they didn't need to see me or even communicate with me at all (which served her objectives perfectly). Once you put your children in a position of control, the entire parent-child dynamic begins to crumble.

It became a horrible vicious cycle. I would text Brooke that I would be coming to see her at my appointed time on Sunday, and she would text back that she didn't want to see me that weekend because of other plans. I would then text back that it wasn't her choice to *not* see me for the few hours I was allotted each week according to the visitation schedule. She would then reply that she didn't like that I was getting angry and that she definitely wouldn't see me. It was more maddening than I can accurately express, especially since it was obvious that every text that I sent was being read, dissected, and answered by the committee of Brooke, Diane, and possibly Dave. It seemed like me against the world.

The most maddening aspect was that Brooke was now essentially my parent. She would only respond when she wanted to, and most of the time she wouldn't respond at all. I haven't experienced anything worse, even prison, than having my twelve-year-old daughter treat me like a classmate that she didn't respect. This is the girl I gave life to, whose diapers I changed regularly, who I held when she was sick, and who I helped get to sleep at night. I loved her more than anything else in the world besides her sister, and she was now treating me like I was an annoying cousin who could be ignored with impunity. I was religiously paying for her financial support and her private Catholic school education in addition to saving over $100,000 for her college education. It particularly bothered me that I was paying almost $5,000 a year for her to attend a Catholic school where they were teaching moral lessons such as "Honor your father and mother." This certainly wasn't translating very well to her treatment of me, her father. It was as heartbreaking as it was emotionally exasperating.

    I also started to realize how emotionally unhealthy this was for Brooke. Obviously it was not a healthy situation for anyone. Especially not a twelve-year-old girl who's been given the power to control her relationship with her father and choose to use this power to blatantly disrespect me and at times actually reprimand me. How could she mature over time in an emotionally healthy way? Deep down I knew that most of the problems resided in Diane's manipulation and control, but that didn't make me feel any better nor miss Brooke any less. And it was certainly no less maddening. Kids tend to model their parents' behavior, and Diane's methodical and calculated efforts to make me look as bad as possible to the girls was working extremely well. Why should they respect me if it was obvious Diane didn't?

It was around this time that I started to ponder some of the many confounding circumstances that a divorce can create. Specifically, as a non-divorced parent, if my child exhibits unacceptable behavior (for example, if she lies to me or ignores an instruction I've given her) and I send her to her room for an hour with the instruction to think about what she has done wrong, I would generally be lauded as a good parent. However, if I'm a divorced dad and the same circumstance occurs, I may very well be labeled an abusive father. My child may claim that I made her upset and use that as an excuse to stop seeing me. Who is really in control in a situation like this? In a perfect world, both parents would be able to handle this together so that the child received the proper message ("I love you, but that behavior is unacceptable"), but realistically, how many divorced parents are emotionally able to work together to bring about a useful result, especially when personality disorders are involved?

Studies have shown that children of broken homes have more difficulties as adults than their peers from non-divorced families. Given the double standard in the above example, is it any wonder that's the case? Until issues such as these are addressed through increased sensitivity by parents, attorneys, counselors, and the court system, many children and parents will continue to struggle with the realities of divorce.

My counselor suggested I try to apologize to the girls for my role in making them uncomfortable by losing patience and sometimes getting angry. The hope was that, by assuring them that I understood that my getting upset wasn't helping things and that I would be aware of that in the future, they would appreciate my honesty and try to work with me to make things better. With that objective, I wrote the following email and sent it to both of them.

> Laurie and Brooke,
>
> I want to apologize for letting my anger affect my relationship with both of you. It was wrong, and I am very sorry.
>
> I miss you both very much – you were the center of my life for many years. I haven't handled being apart from you guys very well. And I've let my anger at your mom affect the way I've interacted with you both.
>
> Trust is very important in life, and I know I've undermined your trust in me. That will change now. You both trusted me for many years, and, despite the past few months, you can trust me now. I am proud of the dad I was to both of you.
>
> Even though it came time for our lives as a family to end, I never intended to break the bond we had with each other.
>
> I was very disappointed at how little I heard from either of you once we separated, and I never anticipated that would be the result of the divorce. But I also know I was responsible for some of that as well. The more I missed you, the angrier I got, and I let my anger affect my behavior towards you guys, which obviously made things worse.

I hope you feel that life is better with a dad you can talk to and spend time with. I know life is better with two great daughters.

Love

Dad

I tried to carefully state my apology in a way that was as genuine as the feelings I'd always had for them. And I hoped they would start interacting in a way that gave us the ability to move forward unshackled from the past several months that had been so poisonous. I specifically hoped that Brooke would stop her efforts to control my ability to see her.

My hopes faded quickly. I never got a response from either girl.

The risk I took by sending that email was that anything less than a positive result would deepen my pain and therefore make things worse. And that's exactly what happened. It seemed to me now that the girls were being just as heartless and manipulative as Diane. Even my counselor was shocked at my getting no response.

Around this time I went to Brooke's Catholic elementary school and met with the principal there (who I've known for several years). I sat in her office and requested she bring Brooke down to her office so I could tell her I loved her and to give her a hug. I asked the principal to stay in the office with us to confirm everything was appropriate. The principal told me that she could not do that, and cited school policy.

Unbelievably, she told me that unless I could prove to her that I had legal custody at that moment she would not let me talk to my own daughter. What's the likelihood that Diane was asked for proof of anything when she was at the school? Given the private tuition I was paying for Brook to attend that school I found it even further infuriating that I was being obstructed from seeing her there. I could understand if there was some kind of legal order restricting me from seeing my daughter, but that certainly wasn't the case. What could be more appropriate at a Catholic school than a parent telling his child how much he loves her?

Of all the hurtful experiences so far with the girls, the worst was yet to come. Since Laurie is six years older than Brooke, the relationship we had together had existed for a longer period of time and was hopefully a bit stronger. Despite the typical teenage rebellious attitude, which wasn't a big issue with Laurie, we had shared some special times together, including the walks we took and our time together visiting colleges. I was still very proud that Laurie was heading to college shortly and had been thinking of what it would feel like to have her leave for her freshman year.

Laurie had chosen the college she would attend, and it was a good school within a couple hours of the town we lived. I was especially proud that she got accepted at such a good school, and it was also the school I secretly felt was the best suited for her personality in terms of size and location.

As the summer edged to a close, I realized that I needed to broach the subject of how she would move onto campus and who would be involved in the process. I so much wanted to move her since I was the one who took her to visit the school and had talked so many times with her about college in general. I also still chafed at the thought that Diane had withdrawn $18,000 from my 529 plan for Laurie after we separated, which I still felt was one of the most obvious acts of selfishness Diane had ever displayed. On top of it all, it was I who had set up the 529 plans for the girls (in my name) and had earned and funded every dollar in both plans.

Unfortunately, I had let my hopes get too high, which set me up for a big crash. Laurie told me she decided that Diane would move her onto campus, which meant that Dave would be there as well. The fact that Dave, who had shunned his own girls and conspired with Diane to file a false police report to get me arrested and imprisoned, was going to be involved in moving my oldest child to college while I stayed home and wrote the checks angered me beyond belief. To me, this was a betrayal beyond anything I had ever considered. It hurt me on so many levels that I couldn't even think about it without getting extremely emotional.

The day I knew she was packing and leaving for school was a hellish time. I was nauseous all that day and the next. Laurie promised me that she'd invite me to go to a football game together a couple of weeks after school started. That seemed like a small concession on her part and actually turned out to be even more hurtful when I walked into her dorm room to find a large collage of pictures on the wall near her bed. All the pictures were of her mom, Brooke, and her friends, and right in the middle was a handwritten note: "Laurie, you can become anything you dream of being. Love, Dave." There wasn't one damn picture of me—me, the man who had made her whole life possible and was paying every damn penny for her to be there. It felt like another betrayal, one which will take a while for me to recover from.

As I would soon find out, the betrayals were just beginning. Late in the fall semester, Laurie told me that she had contacted one of the other colleges she had originally applied to about the possibility of transferring there for the spring semester. She was happily surprised to get a positive response from the school and ultimately was accepted as a transfer student in the spring. I was very supportive of her decision since it was another very fine school. Once again, though, I got my hopes up that I might be the one to move her there, especially since it seemed more than fair given that Diane and Dave moved her on campus in the fall. Once again, I was bitterly disappointed as she refused me the opportunity to help with the move. Diane and Dave got to move her to the school, as I again paid the bills—all the bills, that is, until she contacted me saying that she needed several hundred dollars for her books for the spring semester. I had been psychologically abused far too much to simply acquiesce. I sent her an angry email in response, telling her she could find a way to pay for her own books and that maybe she should ask Diane and Dave to pay for them since they were the only ones getting to enjoy the things I'd had always dreamed of enjoying when my daughter went off to college.

What little satisfaction I got from that bit of defiance was short-lived since not long afterwards I received a letter from Diane's attorney stating that she had met with my daughter Laurie and was now representing her as well. The letter stated I was to have no further communication with Laurie regarding her college costs and that I was from then on only to deal with the attorney. They were planning legal action against me, claiming that I was mismanaging my 529 plan for Laurie by failing to pay for Laurie's books. My own daughter had obtained legal representation against me to ensure that I paid every penny for her college education in the exact amounts she wanted.

It turns out I hadn't fully realized what betrayal could actually mean or how much it could actually hurt.

Chapter 10

Moving Away

Adding to my everyday stress was the realization that Diane and Dave were not opposed to filing a false police report to achieve their objectives, and therefore I was only one devious lie away (by either or both of them) from going to prison. The judge had made it abundantly clear that the next time I showed up in his courtroom, prison was where I was headed. It still greatly bothers me that he never seemed concerned about the veracity of the claims against me or the truth in general. He saw an attractive woman in his court claiming she was frightened, and that was good enough for him. I was guilty in his eyes regardless of any evidence to the contrary.

My counselor and I talked about this stressful reality several times, and she seemed as genuinely shaken by the prospect of me going to prison as I was. Finally, she suggested something that I probably would never have considered myself. I should consider moving away from central Pennsylvania. My first reaction was that I wasn't going to let Diane and Dave force me to move away from Brooke. Even though I wasn't seeing much of Brooke, I still felt some connection to her given that I was living in the same house we had lived in together for seven years, plus it would be a bit of a disruption for my business. I certainly wasn't inclined to seriously consider moving away.

I started to notice, however, that every time I'd hear a car door close while I was home, I'd feel a surge of panic. Was it the police coming to arrest me again? I was now so psychologically abused that I expected Diane and Dave to make sure I somehow spent more time in prison. My life no longer seemed under my control. I felt that if I accidentally saw either of them anywhere in public, all Diane would need to do was to say that I "glared' at her." The most outrageous aspect of my case was that there was no burden on Diane to prove I had glared at her (other than to have Dave corroborate), and I certainly knew there was no way for me to prove I *hadn't* glared at her. What the hell is a glare in the legal sense anyway? To the judge it seemed that a glare was whatever Diane said it was. It's a very scary thought to know that you are guilty whenever people as disturbed as Diane and Dave say you are. The concept of innocent until proven guilty doesn't seem to apply to restraining orders in that central Pennsylvania courthouse. It's simply too easy to justify outrageous legal abuse by lumping everything under the heading of "domestic violence" in order to protect women. Some women are much more capable of abusive behavior than their husband or ex-spouse will ever be. Making up lies to get your ex-spouse thrown in prison is much more heinous and dangerous behavior than any 'glare'.

My counselor eventually convinced me that I'd have more control over my life and eliminate Diane's manipulation by moving away. At that point, I wouldn't consider moving anywhere in Pennsylvania. If the legal system in central Pennsylvania was anything like the rest of the state, I wanted no part of staying there. I had no experience as a defendant in any other jurisdiction, so I can't say my fears of kangaroo justice elsewhere in the state were a legitimate concern, but I certainly wasn't going to take any chances.

Attorneys and police officers I have spoken with in Pennsylvania were all unanimous in their opinion that restraining orders are much too easy to get and are many times too harshly enforced. The burden of proof to file for a restraining order in non-violent situations is disturbingly low. To get a temporary restraining order requires little or no proof. In my opinion, if the accused has a clean criminal record and no previous domestic violence issues, the judge should be very cautious, realizing that claims and counterclaims are easy to make in the tense emotional atmosphere surrounding divorce and domestic situations in general. Otherwise, it's possible that domestic violence operates in reverse. Everyone's rights should be protected, not just the rights of an attractive woman who may actually be a wolf in sheep's clothing.

One potential solution is that anyone filing a report of a restraining order violation against someone with no history of violence or previous criminal record be required to pass a polygraph test if the parties involved offer reasonably different versions of an event. Because a restraining order gives a devious accuser enormous potential to control and harass, I don't think passing a polygraph test is an unreasonable hurdle to clear to validate a violation. I wonder how many restraining order violations, probation orders, and prison stays would never have occurred if this were the case. I'm confident that Diane would not have passed any polygraph challenge to her claim that I blocked the front door with my car and glared at her for three minutes. The playing field in such instances would be much more level, with everyone's constitutional rights more likely protected.

After considering the pros and cons of moving away from Pennsylvania, I decided to take my counselor's advice and leave. Brooke was refusing to see me on a regular basis, and Laurie was at college, so I really had nothing to gain by staying if I wanted to sleep soundly at night and know I was beyond the reach of Diane and Dave. I chafed, though, at the thought of how crazy it was that I was paying thousands of dollars monthly in alimony, child support, and other expenses to Diane while feeling the need to leave the state because she was, legally, in a position to continue to harass me. It seemed insane, as if the inmates were running the asylum.

After spending a couple of months analyzing my professional opportunities in the mid-Atlantic region, I decided that moving to northern Virginia was my best option. I put my house up for sale and within three months left Pennsylvania.

A few months after I moved to Virginia, I got a call from a friend in Pennsylvania who told me she noticed that Dave had put his house up for sale. It didn't take a genius to deduce that it was more than likely that he and Diane planned to at least cohabitate, and maybe even marry. Our separation agreement provided for me to stop paying alimony in either scenario. I obviously had a significant interest in what they might have planned. I had my attorney send an email to Diane's attorney inquiring as to any plans Diane had concerning living with Dave. I wasn't naïve enough to believe that they might tell me something I didn't have a right to know, but I didn't expect her attorney to conspire with Diane or tell a bald-faced lie. Within the next week we received two separate responses from Diane's attorney, which included the information excerpted here.

On June 4th:

Diane is not cohabitating. She would, however, like to remarry and expects that to occur by the end of next year. Richard will be among the first to know of a date certain, as well as any intentions she has to cohabitate.

On June 6th:

Even though Diane hopes to remarry, there is no date certain, and there's no guarantee that it will even occur.

Based on these representations by Diane's attorney, my own attorney and I made some decisions that resulted in my paying Diane $4,500 in return for concessions and amendments to our separation agreement. The date of the final agreement addendum was July 17th.

Unbelievably, I again got a call from a friend who said that it seemed Dave had moved from his house. I asked my attorney to email Diane's attorney to clarify whether any cohabitation was taking place. Diane's attorney's responded with the following.

> "Per your request, it is my understanding that Diane married on July 20th and the marriage license was pulled on the 11th."

After all the denials from Diane's attorney, Diane actually remarried *only three days* after I sent her $4,500 for the addendum I thought we were negotiating in good faith. She and her attorney flatly lied to me and my attorney for financial gain. I wasn't surprised that Diane would lie, but I was upset that her attorney seemed to have conspired in the deception. Her attorney refused to provide any feedback when questioned about the obvious discrepancy between her multiple emails denying any immediate intent of Diane to remarry or cohabitate and the fact that Diane remarried and cohabitated only days afterwards.

I believe that attorneys, like all professionals, should be held to a reasonable ethical standard, and it concerns me that Diane's attorney may have failed to meet a reasonable standard given the misleading information she provided on multiple occasions. Then again, it's possible that she too was a victim of Diane's untrustworthiness.

Moving Away

It's clear that Diane will never stop her efforts to take advantage of me in any way she possibly can, and it's an open question as to whether she is even capable of any other behavior given her personality disorder.

As the end of the summer neared, my thoughts again turned to Laurie heading back to college. I was still reeling from her decision to retain an attorney against me regarding her college payments. I had no delusions that she would allow me to be involved in moving her back to campus, but I wanted to reach out to her and give her some well-wishes and thoughts that might be helpful to her over the next few years. Here's what I sent via email.

Hi Laurie

As you get ready to head back to school, I wanted to put some things in writing to you. I have no idea whether you will read this, but regardless, it helps me to know I tried to communicate with you and provide some of my thoughts.

I know what it's like to go to college and the anxieties and unknowns involved. I also understand you pretty well and the ways you internalize a lot of things which cause stress for you. I've been there. In many ways, those unknowns you're experiencing now are what life ends up being about—unknown opportunities, anxieties, happiness, unhappiness, love, regret, etc. Most importantly it's best to learn that pushing yourself outside your comfort zone is where you'll find the most happiness and ultimately where you'll find "yourself." When you're young it seems so important to find someone special and create structure, but looking back, that's really more a way of playing it safe and avoiding the stress of the unknown. There's good stress and bad stress. Learning to handle the stress of exploring your potential as a person is likely to be the most important factor in your ultimate happiness. I've learned happiness isn't a destination as much as a willingness to open yourself to the stress of the journey in a way which enables you to be increasingly confident that you have the tools necessary to cope with the bad times and enjoy the good times.

Some people turn to drugs, sex, alcohol, etc., but these things just provide false hope and short-term relief. Life is unfair in many ways, and people are born with different capabilities of handling stress, etc. I never found it easy to be outgoing, adventurous, overly confident or assertive, but I learned over time that as I made the effort to do/be those things that they became less stressful and more natural to me. I think you are that way as well, and I encourage you to keep making the effort to move outside your comfort zone, where ultimate happiness is much more likely.

Ultimately, the best skill you can develop is to get as comfortable as possible interacting with other people. Almost everything you will want or need to accomplish in your life will be a function of developing the ability to communicate and develop relationships with others (in some cases learning to be as tolerant as possible is the best you can do). What I've realized as I get older is that the ability to relate well to others is very much a function of how you feel about yourself and your ability to feel good about yourself regardless of the feedback you may get (or more likely falsely perceive) from others along the way. There are so many great people to meet, but there are lots of idiots too. The trick is to minimize the effect the idiots have on you and maximize the effect the people have who are truly nice, honest, and trustworthy. Please also remember that one-way streets always result in dead-ends. The best relationships are those that are mutually beneficial, which means you need to be confident enough to add value to others as well.

I do need to say some things about my marriage because it may help you understand and learn from the mistakes I made. This is not to blame anyone but myself. I made all the choices myself and I think it supports a lot of what I've said above: I wanted so much to be a dad that I ignored some very significant warning signs. The fact that we had you so quickly (literally a honeymoon baby) was very exciting. But looking back I was never truly in love with your mom. Our backgrounds were so different, and I was too focused on creating a family. The truth is I knew after the first year of our marriage that I had made a huge mistake, but I loved being your dad. Getting married to anyone is a crapshoot under the best of circumstances, but wanting to start a family is the wrong reason to overlook issues that you're clearly uncomfortable with. After some counseling, I have realized that the behavior I put up with during the marriage from your mom was a significant form of abuse, and I now understand why I felt so horrible and was so unhappy. Regardless though, for seventeen years I focused on you girls. As you know, I was always around for each of you and provided a good example of what a loving father should be to his kids.

The biggest thing I learned was to never stay around people you don't trust, and for God's sake please don't marry someone you don't trust.

Speaking of trust, I need to specifically address our relationship. We have no trust between us at all. I understand why you feel you can't trust me, but you need to understand the ways you've betrayed me. I have seen a couple of professional counselors (as I've told you) and have received their feedback along the way. I won't belabor this issue, but please understand that they have been appalled at your behavior toward me.

I miss you and Brooke very much, but I've had no choice but to move on and become a happy person. In the process of moving to Virginia to avoid the hurtful behavior of you, Brooke, and your mom towards me, I have become a fairly happy person, and it gets better each day. Being away from your mom has enabled me to gain a new perspective on what it's like to trust people and genuinely care again.

We will never have the relationship a father and daughter should have. We are past that point now. But it is possible for us to be friends someday. I will try to be as supportive as I can if it turns out we can get on terms that are mutually agreeable/acceptable. I truly hope we can.

I never got any response from Laurie and therefore don't know if she even read it. But I felt good having sent it to her.

Regarding Brooke, as of this writing I have not seen or spoken with her in twenty months. She, like Laurie, has blocked me from her Facebook page in an attempt to eliminate me entirely from her life. I only ever sent her one Facebook message, several months ago, when I saw a recent picture of her: "You are as beautiful as you are in my dreams." Shortly thereafter, I was blocked from her page. I know nothing about her life.

I don't hear from my girls on Thanksgiving, Christmas, or worst of all, on Father's Day, nor do they respond when I text them on those days. I continue to pay all the financial support I am obligated to pay, as I always have. I miss my girls. and I love them, as I always have and always will.

Both Diane and Dave testified against me at a recent custody hearing, claiming that seeing me would upset Brooke.

PART 2

Chapter 11

Narcissistic Personality Disorder

While I noticed some of Diane's disturbing personality issues during our marriage, it never occurred to me that some of her behaviors were diagnosable as recognized disorders, which can make living together successfully a difficult challenge. I also would have thought, maybe correctly, that we all have some degree of dysfunctional behavior that makes us difficult at times—idiosyncrasies that make us all special and unique.

I've learned, however, that personality disorders are more than idiosyncrasies. Psychological disorders are more pervasive dysfunctions that typically constitute a noticeable pattern over a prolonged period of time. In Diane's case, her neighborhood nickname of *comandante* was an early indication that she had control tendencies that extended beyond the range of normal assertive behavior.

Once my counselors informed me that Diane's behavior indicated textbook narcissistic patterns, I started to read articles on narcissism and specifically how narcissism affects marriage and divorce. It was helpful to begin to understand the typical traits that narcissist's exhibit, but again, it seemed to me that all of us at times exhibit these traits to one degree or another. I learned as I read further that the important issue is how pervasive the traits are and the degree to which they lead to dysfunction.

A useful summary of typical characteristics of a narcissist include:

- Has a need for admiration

- A need to be right

- A need to be seen as the good guy

- A need to criticize when you don't meet their needs

- Is charismatic and successful

- Lacks the ability to feel remorse

- Has no conscience

- Has a tremendous need to control you and the situation

- Uses a facade of caring and understanding to manipulate

- Is emotionally unavailable
- Nothing is ever their fault
- Hangs onto resentment
- Has a grandiose sense of self
- Feels misunderstood
- Is not interested in solving marital problems; it is their way or the highway
- Is envious of other's success

My initial reaction was to go down this list to determine if I myself was the narcissist. Maybe *I* was the problem. I took some of the information I had found to my counselor and presented this possibility to her, and she assured me that being a narcissist wasn't something I need to worry about. That was nice to know.

It was very telling, however, that Diane's behavior and personality were so accurately outlined by the list. Many of the issues I had noticed and tolerated over our seventeen-year marriage were clearly defined. Particularly accurate were her need for absolute control, lack of remorse, and a grandiose sense of self. These were things I remember as very significant sources of aggravation and consternation for me and were therefore problematical for the marriage. The more information I found, the more I was able to understand what I was up against.

It became clear, for example, that the patterns of control that Diane exhibited during the marriage had manifested themselves in the divorce process as well, and especially as they pertained to the custody of our girls. Given the nature of divorce itself, which is inherently emotional and unsettling, someone with narcissistic tendencies will likely fight all attempts at compromise. One thing that always stood out to me about Diane during our time together was that she never seemed capable of true compromise. As I've previously stated, whatever she didn't win for herself was considered a loss. The concept of win-win never occurred to her.

Her constant threats to take me to court if I didn't agree to give her a greater percentage of our assets, together with her decision to take $18,000 from my college savings plan for Laurie, are obvious examples of her need to gain more for herself than would be normal. In hindsight, I should have gone to divorce court since narcissists don't have control in that setting and are therefore forced to compromise by legal mandate. If I were to give anyone advice who might be involved in a divorce with someone with narcissistic tendencies, it would be to move the process to an impartial setting, such as court or arbitration, regardless of the costs involved. The results are likely to be more equitable, and the process will almost certainly be more civil than if the narcissist is able to exert the control he or she craves.

When I commented to my counselor about how disappointed I was that Diane had jumped so immediately into a serious relationship with Dave, resulting in a lack of transition for the girls after our having been a family for so long, she pointed out that Diane's decision to quickly find someone new also fit the narcissistic pattern. It was a way for her to exert control by using the addition of another man as a means of obscuring my role as their dad and diverting their attention from the past. Also, Diane likely lived in fear that I would develop a serious relationship with a woman who would also have influence over the girls. Any woman introduced to the girls would be seen by Diane as diminishing her control and influence over them, and that possibility was certainly unacceptable to her.

As I read more about the dynamics of narcissism, I learned that narcissists who get divorced tend to discount the value of the original family unit. They have the ability to move quickly to another relationship because they don't feel there was any previous value to protect. Everything they focus on revolves around themselves, and it never occurs to them that keeping and nurturing some useful family memories from the past would be in the best interest of the kids. Instead, they are only focused on their current attempts to control the kids' attention by creating new realities in the form of new relationships and experiences. To Diane, I not only became expendable as a dad to the girls, but she saw me as a threat to her efforts to control the girls' attention and environment. Fortunately for her, Dave was a willing participant in the effort to entertain my girls instead of honoring my custody time with them. I found it reprehensible that any man (particularly a divorced man) would become involved in arranging activities for kids when they are scheduled for visitations with their father. I can never forgive Dave for his lack of respect for my right to be with my daughters.

It also made sense, in the context of narcissism, that Diane purchased an expensive townhouse at the time we separated even though she had no job and wasn't likely to generate much of her own income in the near future. She felt she deserved to be in a more expensive area of town. Where she lived, where she vacationed, and who she socialized with were her overriding concerns. I allowed her to enjoy the lifestyle she craved, both before and after the divorce. I look back at the fact that I was living on savings for a while in order to pay for her lifestyle and realize now how I created many of my own problems. But with my girls living mainly at Diane's townhouse, nothing was an unemotional decision. I certainly suffered a great deal from my mistakes. The alternative, however, was that my girls may have suffered more than they did if I hadn't made things quite so easy for Diane. Whether that is actually true or not I'll never know, but it definitely makes me feel better to think that way.

Although I wasn't overly confident that our marriage counseling was going to lead to a significant improvement in our relationship, I certainly was supportive of any process that included an objective third party to help clarify issues and identify weak areas in our marriage. As it turns out, the counseling wasn't very helpful, and in the context of Diane's Narcissistic Personality Disorder, I shouldn't have been optimistic that it would. As noted, narcissists rarely admit that anything is their fault. They have such a high regard for themselves that mistakes tend to be regarded as the other person's fault. This attitude enables them to control others through guilt. I can distinctly remember our counselor asking Diane to stop identifying things she felt I was doing wrong and to focus on her own behavior, and yet it always seemed to come back to things she felt she deserved and wasn't getting. The marriage counselor made a significant and obvious effort to get Diane to realize that being a stay-at-home mom who went out frequently with her girlfriends, one who took vacations away from the family, was unusually fortunate (or, in my opinion, unusually selfish) compared to many women who need to work outside the home against their preference.

In the context of Narcissistic Personality Disorder, it's easier now for me to understand the absurd arguments Diane and I had about issues such as why it wasn't appropriate for her to be in bars until after midnight on a regular basis with her girlfriends, or why, as a married woman, dancing with male strippers was seen as offensive and inappropriate by her husband. At the time I felt as if I were in an alternate universe, and everyone could see the realities of Diane's destructive behavior but her. I now have a better understanding that she doesn't perceive things from the same perspective as most people. Since an important narcissistic characteristic is a lack of empathy for others, she naturally didn't care how I felt about her stripper escapades or her drunken flirting.

It was also ridiculous how she would demand equal time out with her girlfriends after the few times every year I would have dinner with a guy in the neighborhood for a couple of hours, always returning home before nine o'clock. Her need to make plans with her girlfriends simply because I had dinner with a friend was almost juvenile. The "me first" attitude that is characteristic of Narcissistic Personality Disorder is a big obstacle to making a relationship work in the long run.

While I've learned to understand some of the issues involved, I certainly don't recommend that anyone subordinate his happiness to accommodate the unrealistic expectations of a narcissistic partner. I believed for a long time that things were my fault and that I was the selfish one even though the evidence suggested just the opposite. But you can lose your soul by letting yourself cater to the happiness of your partner at the long-term expense of your own. I would never do it again.

Finally, maybe the worst effect Diane's narcissism had on me was her decision to bring our daughter Brooke into court in order to testify to false accusations against me. This is also what my counselor found the most appalling. Diane's objective was to make sure I had almost no chance to gain significant custody of Brooke, and she and Dave knew getting me arrested would help achieve that objective. Did she care if there were long- term effects that might affect Brooke for many years? Did she consider that doing things that were illegal, immoral, and unethical was against a common code of conduct? Did she have any trouble sleeping at night afterwards? I'm sure the answer is "no". She clearly found ways to justify all of it, in the same way she justified having me arrested (by telling the girls she had no choice in the matter because otherwise she'd be in legal peril herself).

I am now trying to access and understand any information which is useful to me going forward. My goal now is to integrate that knowledge into my ongoing efforts to gain a relationship with my girls. I'm fighting a very difficult battle because Diane will never see things in the context of what is best for our daughters.

I'm not sure how the knowledge I have now about the narcissistic personality may have helped me during my marriage. My guess is that I may have ended my marriage sooner than I did because I would more quickly have lost all hope of Diane changing in any way that would be productive. Whether ending the relationship sooner would have helped anything isn't a question I'll ever be able to answer. I think it's likely that it would have robbed me of even more time with the girls. In that sense, I'm glad I didn't know then what I know now.

But I definitely would have handled the divorce differently had I known about Diane's narcissism. Given the understanding that she was going to be irrational from the start, I would have cared much less about paying attorney's fees and much more about making sure I had as much leverage as possible to counteract her unrealistic expectations and constant legal threats.

Recommended Books:

"Stop Walking on Eggshells – Taking Your Life Back When Someone You Care About Has Borderline Personality Disorder" by Paul T. Mason, M.S. and Randi Kreger

"Disarming the Narcissist – Surviving and Thriving with the Self-Absorbed" by Wendy T. Behary, LCSW

Chapter 12

Parental Alienation Syndrome

The most crushing blow I endured as a result of my divorce has been the loss of my relationship with my girls. Ironically, my relationship with them was the only happy aspect of my marriage, and they were the reason I tolerated Diane's abuse for so long.

It was obvious from the early days of our separation that Diane was purposely attempting to minimize my role as a parent. She skillfully reduced my role to that of providing financial support and made sure the girls were aware of what my financial responsibilities were. By exaggerating what these financial obligations actually were, she was able to portray me as a deadbeat dad in eyes of the girls. This is especially egregious since I had agreed to pay significantly more than I would have if I had mounted a legal battle in court. I also have never missed a required support payment.

Laurie's email to me after I refused to give her my credit card number (although I didn't refuse to pay the college application fees) represented the first occasion that I realized just how effective Diane's efforts were and the point at which I realized that my relationship with my daughters was slipping away. It was the moment I had feared, beginning with my initial thoughts about getting a divorce. It's a very scary prospect when someone you do not trust (and who has little or no social or moral conscience) becomes your adversary. Although I had hoped for the best, deep down I knew that a harmonious family life after divorce, one in which I would play a significant role, was unlikely with Diane. But I never thought that she could bring about the results she wanted as skillfully and quickly as she did. But then again, I made it much easier for her given the mistakes I made and the anger I let get the better of me.

As I've now learned as a result of extensive reading and speaking with professionals, Parental Alienation Syndrome is the term used to describe the efforts of one parent to undermine the relationship a child has with the other parent. Because children are quite impressionable, many will eventually succumb to the relentless programming, or "brainwashing," by the alienating parent. At the time of my divorce, I had no idea that such a behavioral pattern existed, nor would I have ever thought that my girls would have been susceptible to efforts to put a wedge between them and me. In my mind, our relationship was much too strong. It now seems to me that the most insidious aspect of the efforts to alienate a parent from children is how effective it can be regardless of the strength of the bond that may have previously existed with the kids.

The pattern of alienation, once initiated by the adult, tends to be copied by children, who have no real understanding as to why they are acting in inappropriate ways. This is greatly facilitated when the child spends significantly more time with the parent who has the intent of causing the alienation. In my case, Diane had custody of the girls at least eighty percent of the time because of my need to be the primary financial support for the separated family. It galls me that my ability and willingness to enable Diane to be a stay-at-home mom reduced her earning potential so that I had a larger financial burden at the time of divorce. This limited my availability to be with the girls post-divorce, which in turn gave Diane more time to poison their attitudes towards me.

Although parental alienation is not specific to one gender, it's seems that the majority of alienation efforts are against men. Given that most divorces result in women having majority custody, men have less time to foster post-divorce relationships with their kids and therefore have less ability to combat any alienation efforts by their ex-spouses. Although it was not true in my situation, men typically enter into dating relationships far more quickly than women after divorce, which can serve as a trigger in many cases for the ex-wife to try and exert undue control.

I've had many interesting discussions recently about decisions couples make concerning issues such as whether one parent will stay at home full-time. This option isn't as feasible as it once was, with two-income households being the norm, and therefore can be a real loss for both the parent and the child. But given that at least half of marriages end in divorce, it might be wise to factor in ramifications of a potential separation as you make decisions before and during the marriage. I've had discussions with several women who expressed regret regarding their poor financial positions post-divorce since they gave up careers to stay at home. I'm not advocating one choice over the other, but decisions either way can have significant ramifications down the road.

While I don't regret allowing Diane to stay home for the girls, I do regret giving Diane a relatively comfortable lifestyle that served to inhibit my ability to have more custody of the girls after the divorce. If Diane had worked and had an income, the financial burden of our post-divorce reality would have been shared more equally and I could have had a more equitable custody arrangement. Although the idea of considering divorce arrangements while you're young and madly in love may seem distasteful, it's not much different from pre-nuptial financial arrangements many people now routinely use.

There are likely many reasons a parent will try to inhibit or sever a child's relationship with the other parent. Any parent who has exhibited controlling behavior during the marriage would likely pose a higher risk for precipitating damaging behavior post-divorce. People in marriages in which control and abuse are obvious pre-divorce factors may need to get counselors involved in the early stages of the separation in order to identify and discuss possible dysfunctional behaviors. In my case, I can't say we could have done anything that would have affected the outcome as I've described it, but I know it would have been prudent to try. At the very least, I might have found a way to control my angry reactions in situations that were made worse by releasing my pent-up aggravation.

It also stands to reason that spouses with narcissistic issues are at much higher risk for exhibiting unhealthy behavior in order to alienate the other parent. In that sense, again, I wish I had understood Diane's issues early enough to get some professional guidance as to ways I might have structured things to help the kids be less susceptible to Diane's manipulation.

Based on what I've read about Parental Alienation Syndrome, it seems that people who come from dysfunctional family structures are at greater risk of demonstrating behavior that would fit the classification of parental alienation. This certainly makes sense on the surface, and it applied to Diane and me. Neither of us had an ideal upbringing, and Diane had significant challenges with the early loss of her father and her mother's emotional issues.

My constant worry is how Diane's successful efforts to remove me from the girls' lives and replace me with Dave will affect them as they mature. It's clear to me that Laurie has subsequently exhibited behavior that is extremely out of character from the girl I knew and loved. I still cringe at the thought of her email to me justifying my arrests and pointing out my financial obligations. I can't imagine a circumstance that would have made me act that way towards my father. The basic respect that I deserve as her father no longer existed from Laurie's perspective. She clearly chose sides, a move that came completely out of the blue and blindsided me with severe emotional force. Even now, I get emotional thinking about how disoriented I became from reading her words and the feelings I had of pure betrayal.

    I've learned that many of the parents who exhibit typical behavior involved in alienation efforts are sociopaths and therefore may not be able to stop acting in such harmful ways. Sociopaths are generally considered to be incapable of having empathy, sympathy, or compassion for others. Therefore, a sociopathic ex-spouse who gives no consideration to the entitlements of the other parent and does not consider the best interests of the children will have a greater likelihood of creating harmful situations. I'm no expert, but there is likely a correlation between sociopathic behavior and narcissistic tendencies. One may well feed the other, and I believe this is the case with Diane. The speed with which she exerted control over the girls and then justified her behavior to them clearly demonstrates the lack of a moral compass, and a warped social conscience.

    It's extremely hurtful to see and feel your kids pull away from you. It's not a natural occurrence, particularly when it happens over a very short period of time. It's hard for most divorced people to transition from being a married spouse to a single person, and from being a full-time mom or dad to a part-time parent almost overnight. Nothing was harder for me, and I knew all along it would be gut-wrenching. I knew it would be hard even when I assumed that my relationship with my girls would be as solid as it had always been. I never even considered that I'd go from a being family of four to an island of one. I felt thrown away, expendable in a way that my heart wasn't prepared for.

I would like to become an advocate in some capacity for parents who are victims of Parental Alienation Syndrome (PAS), and particularly to help facilitate the right to bring civil lawsuits against offending spouses. I find it absolutely mind-boggling that such civil suits are not allowed in the vast majority of states. What is more important than a parent's relationship with his or her children? In my case, I spent seventeen years as an attentive father, but I currently have no relationship with either of my daughters. Nothing in my life as a parent ever took priority over my identity as a dad or my efforts to be a good father. Am I partly to blame for my current circumstance with my girls? Absolutely. Do I deserve to lose my relationship with my girls? Absolutely not.

Is it reasonable that most states currently don't provide the legal ability for someone like me to sue my ex-wife in civil court for the pain and suffering that PAS has caused me? Will my relationship with my girls ever be what it would have been without these hurtful efforts? It's not likely. How much have I lost as a father? How do these losses compare to the other types of emotional suffering for which people are routinely able to bring civil suits?

Most importantly, the right to sue for PAS would provide enormous deterrent value. If I, as a parent, received a letter from an attorney outlining provable parental alienation efforts on my part that would allow my spouse to sue me in civil court for what might be significant damages, I would think seriously about my actions going forward. There may be no greater deterrent than the ability of an alienated parent to take an offending spouse to civil court. And if it truly is a deterrent, the instances of PAS will likely drop. And then who wins? Everyone, but especially the kids in the long run.

I find Diane's lack of any capacity for empathy fueled by her dysfunctional need for control to be the most insidious aspect of her behavior. Can't she imagine what it must be like for me to be without the girls constantly? Does she secretly smile on holidays when, once again, she has them all to herself and knows they aren't even contacting me? I'm very sure she does. And that's how I know she's a very sick person. Having lost her father at such a young age, you might think she would make sure I was a constant resource for the girls, a source of love, affection, advice, and reassurance. But any gain the girls would receive by interaction with me is seen by Diane as her loss since everything essentially comes down to how much control she keeps over every situation.

I will say, too, that it's difficult at times for me not to blame the girls themselves, especially Laurie since she's so much older and had more experiences with me to serve as a moral compass. I'm torn at times between logic that says the girls are merely victims of a very controlling sociopath, and the many gentle and loving moments the girls and I frequently shared that should be as imprinted on their hearts as they are on mine. Maybe I'm simply not capable at this point of the emotional balance required to truly understand.

I dream of the day that both girls will be able to see everything from a wider perspective. It haunts me that all of their experiences now are unbalanced in Diane's favor. Each day seems to me to be another tear in the tether of the heartstrings between them and me. It's unnatural and unhealthy. But I remain hopeful.

Book Recommendations:

"Divorce Poison – How to Protect Your Family from Bad-mouthing and Brainwashing" by Dr. Richard A. WarshaK

"Adult Children of Parental Alienation Syndrome – Breaking the Ties That Bind" by Amy J. L. Baker

Chapter 13

Divorce Related Malicious Parent Syndrome

I recently became fascinated with psychological literature I read by Ira Daniel Turkat, Ph.D. His work identified post-divorce behavioral patterns that are separate from other underlying personality issues or disorders. Since Dr. Turkat's work identifies behavior based on the commonly-experienced emotions involved in divorce, it therefore seems to represent a step towards understanding the psychology of divorces in ways maybe previously misunderstood.

Dr. Turkat originally labeled his work Divorce Related Malicious Mother Syndrome because of the syndrome's strong correlation with female behavior in general. The name of the dysfunctional behavior pattern he identified, however, has subsequently been changed to reflect no specific gender bias - Divorce Related Malicious *Parent* Syndrome. I suspect that many of the dysfunctional issues initially identified as predominately female in nature are to a great degree a function of the dynamics of family structures that result in women usually having the lion's share of custody after divorce. It seems a relatively recent development that men more regularly share at least fifty percent custody (likely due to the prevalence of dual wage couples) so that they have access to their children frequently enough for their own dysfunctional behavior patterns to become evident. It's also possible that being a more involved parent now causes the stresses on men previously shouldered disproportionately by women after divorce. Regardless of the dynamics through which dysfunctional behavior develops, the goal should be to understand it as a means of significantly reducing it.

While gender and abusive post-divorce behavior are not necessarily correlated, there's no question that, in terms of societal focus and media coverage, men are either ignored as victims or are more likely to be identified as the bad actors. Quoting from Dr. Turkat's work, "While the media correctly portrays the difficulties imposed upon women and children by the 'deadbeat dad' phenomenon, the cameras have yet to capture the warfare waged by a select group of mothers against child support paying, law abiding fathers. Every day, attorneys and therapists are exposed to horror stories in which vicious behaviors are lodged against innocent fathers and children. Unfortunately, there are no scientific data on the subject. Similarly, the clinical literature has relatively ignored the problem."

Dr. Turkat identifies the diagnostic criteria for Divorce Related Malicious Parent Syndrome as the following.

A parent who unjustifiably punishes his or her divorcing or divorced spouse by:

- Attempting to alienate their mutual child(ren) from the other parent

- Involving others in malicious actions against the other parent

- Engaging in excessive litigation

The parent specifically attempts to deny the child(ren):

- Regular uninterrupted visitation with the other parent

- Uninhibited telephone access to the other parent

- Participation by the other parent in the child(ren)'s school life and extra-curricular activities

The pattern is pervasive and includes malicious acts towards the other parent, including:

- Lying to the children

- Lying to others

- Violations of law

The disorder is not specifically due to another mental disorder, although a separate mental disorder may co-exist.

What I find fascinating about Dr. Turkat's work is his concrete and comprehensive criteria that facilitate an objective assessment of inappropriate behavior. The natural inclination may be to use this information to assess your ex-spouse's behavior, but the criteria also provide a framework of actions any parent can use to access *their own behavior* to determine whether he or she might be acting inappropriately. If these actions are regularly used in hurtful and dysfunctional circumstances, then obviously they should be avoided if one's goal is to act as appropriately as possible.

Dr. Turkat acknowledges the work of Dr. Richard A. Gardner in coining the term Parental Alienation Syndrome and his work in identifying the behaviors and characteristics involved with the patterns of alienation, but he also specifies how his own work takes a more comprehensive approach. Quoting from Dr. Turkat's work, "While Gardner's pioneering descriptions of the Parental Alienation Syndrome provide an important contribution to our understanding of divorce-related hostilities involving children, the present paper is concerned with a more global abnormality. As noted in the examples provided in the beginning of this manuscript, serious attacks on divorcing husbands take place which are beyond merely manipulating the children. Further, these actions include a willingness by some mothers to violate societal law. Finally, there are mothers who persistently engage in malicious behaviors designed to alienate their offspring from the father despite being unable to successfully cause alienation. In sum, these cases do not meet the criteria for Parental Alienation Syndrome. Nevertheless, they portray a serious abnormality."

What is also interesting about Dr. Turkat's work is how uncannily well his criteria for Divorce Related Malicious Parent Syndrome match the abuses I experienced from Diane. When specifically considering the outlined behavior of "involving others in malicious actions against the other parent," it's easy to see how Dave's actions became so coordinated with Diane's in violating my share of the custody. Knowing Diane as well as I do, it seems likely that she initiated the efforts to involve him in the trips and other functions that took place when Brooke should have been with me. But maybe I'm giving Dave a bit too much credit since his history of ignoring his own girls indicates some level of parental dysfunction and potential personality issues. But it's clear that both Diane and Dave were willing to ignore my right to be with my daughters. This fits another of Dr. Turkat's outlined criteria since Diane denied me regular uninterrupted visitation, and disrupted my ability to even communicate with Brooke by confiscating the cell phone I gave her as a Christmas present.

It doesn't serve any useful purpose for me to enumerate all the ways Diane's behavior correlates with the criteria outlined by Dr. Turkat, but, again, it is amazing how her actions seemingly provide an unfortunate example of Divorce Related Malicious Parent Syndrome.

Another issue worth noting (and one of the most disturbing) was Diane's willingness to violate the law. We are all taught to obey the law. I never had any legal issues other than the ones I experienced after my divorce. As previously detailed, Diane's filing of a false police report claiming that I blocked the front door to the townhouse and that I stayed at the house for three minutes glaring at her was pure fabrication and therefore a clear violation of the law by her (and Dave).

I am hopeful that there will continue to be efforts to address the behavioral patterns of parents who hurt others, especially children. It would be very helpful if counselors and judges were educated about these insidious patterns that undermine the divorce process, which is already too fraught it seems with unhealthy bias and opportunities for manipulation.

Chapter 14

Legal Abuse Syndrome

As I've honestly admitted throughout the book, I have made mistakes. I can accept consequences for those mistakes, but there's a difference between accepting reasonable consequences for mistakes and being abused. The consequences I've endured have been brutal.

I've tried to be objective in determining whether I'm just looking for sympathy by playing the role of a victim or whether I was genuinely subjected to unreasonable circumstances that amount to nothing less than torture. Luckily, I've had the help of some professionals along the way, professionals who have facilitated my ability to understand where reasonable lines are normally drawn, and this has helped me draw conclusions I believe are useful.

One question I've grappled with as I've reflected on the past few years is whether a person who is psychologically and legally abused can be expected to make reasonable decisions or display reasonable behavioral patterns. Maybe I've been a bit too hard on myself for my mistakes. As a self-employed man for twenty-five years, I have accepted responsibility for my actions and exhibited the necessary self-discipline required to make a living. I've never been one to shy away from challenges or make excuses.

But as tough and smart as I've always felt I was, I have been emotionally shattered in ways I never dreamt of. As much as I was a great father, and a good person, I suffered to a degree I thought was only reserved for the hardcore criminals of society. How could this have happened to me? Is my story incredibly unique or do similar things happen to good people everywhere? How can we as a society look at the issues involved in abuses that occur throughout the divorce process and start to take steps to make them much less likely, and help ensure better outcomes are more prevalent?

It's time to seriously start focusing on abuses that are frequently experienced by ex-spouses in order to create awareness of parental alienation, which will hopefully lead to attention and efforts for prevention. This has been a great part of my motivation to write this book. People need to tell their stories in order to create attention. Unfortunately, many emotionally shattered people are doing the best they can to muster the necessary energy and optimism to get through each day. Bigger objectives usually are barely comprehensible.

I was abused for many years because of Diane's narcissistic dysfunction, which helped her believe that whatever made her happy was appropriate. There's no doubt that I enabled her ability to live a lifestyle she felt she was entitled to. I accept the blame for that and accept reasonable consequences, one of which is my divorce. I held on to a family life I truly loved and to a family structure I had always wanted. My girls were my happiness and joy. Nothing has ever come close to the feelings of enlightenment and joy that being their dad provided me. Unfortunately, the loss of my relationship with them hurts in equal proportion to the joy they once gave me.

But the issues involved in my story, and likely in the stories of many others, go well beyond my experiences with Diane. The dysfunction that enables abuse and bad outcomes extends to insensitive or corrupt attorneys, omnipotent police officers, over-zealous district attorneys and prosecutors, and judges who believe they've been anointed as deities to impart their own moral code on lesser human beings. People don't become perfect when they graduate from the police academy or get appointed to the bench, and the power one attains as a prosecutor doesn't automatically make her judgments, biases, and antipathies infallible or irrelevant. We give certain people in our society a great deal of power, but do we ever really focus on the likelihood that many of those people also have disorders, biases, and mental health issues that might make them capable of causing significantly more damage to society than the so-called criminals they are authorized to arrest, prosecute, and judge? (I propose that people in law enforcement at all levels, including judges, be required to have mental health screenings at least every two years……..I, for one, would be fascinated to see the results, especially in central PA).

Should we really be allowing anyone to get a restraining order based on trivial or fabricated claims? If I've done something to hurt you, shouldn't I be required to listen to your point of view, even if there's understandable anger expressed? My story doesn't involve any violence, yet I've been arrested three times and spent ten days in prison because a judge saw an attractive woman claiming that I exhibited violent behavior. People snap and bad things happen, and restraining orders have their place. But they shouldn't be given out as a first reaction to a divorce situation.

Here's an important question: Should an ex-spouse be able to alienate children from the other parent, violate custody, taunt her ex-spouse at custody pick-up times, inhibit the ex-spouse's' ability to communicate with their kids, and then get a restraining order claiming she is afraid that the ex-spouse might be angry? How is that any different than kicking a good-natured dog repeatedly, and then when the dog finally reacts in anger you have it sent to the pound as a potential menace to society. It's truly insane.

As noted, I had police officers come to my house to apologize that they had to arrest me based on a warrant citing an email I sent to Diane (i.e., that I wanted to have a beer with Dave to make things better for my girls). I've had attorneys cite abuses involving restraining orders used as tools for harassment (remember Diane using the restraining order to get me to leave Brooke's basketball function). One attorney told me that if I wanted to inhibit Diane's ability to go to Laurie's high school graduation, I could simply file a temporary restraining order against her stating that I felt she was a threat to me and Laurie (I didn't). Restraining orders are easily obtained and misused.

Another issue that I mentioned previously is how easy it is for a parent to bring a minor child into court as a witness to alleged behavior against an ex-spouse. The fact that Diane brought Brooke into court with the intention of having her testify that I glared at Diane and sat in my car for three minutes is still the most outrageous aspect of my entire hellish experience. It's bad enough that Diane and Dave were willing to do that, but should a prosecutor really allow a child to be taken from school for what could be a lifelong traumatic event? Did anyone question if this was proper for the child? Was a professional counselor consulted to help determine its propriety or potential harm? Was this just another way for Diane to further alienate Brooke from me? Shouldn't a judge have input as to whether a minor child's testimony is absolutely required before the child is brought into court? In my opinion, these are question that beg answers.

I recently came across information on what has been labeled Legal Abuse Syndrome, or LAS. Dr. Karin Huffer, M.S., M.F.T., is doing groundbreaking work in this area and describes LAS as a type of post-traumatic stress disorder (PTSD). Published information includes this description: "Legal abuse refers to abuses associated with both civil and criminal legal action. Abuse can originate from nearly any part of the legal system, including frivolous and vexatious litigants, abuses by law enforcement, incompetent, careless or corrupt attorneys and misconduct from the judiciary itself." I've experienced abuse from all such parties.

It's certainly a positive development that more attention is being paid to the way the legal system can be manipulated in order to inflict harm on ex-spouses, but society is a long way from implementing any meaningful changes. I am appalled by the behavior of Diane's attorneys, who acted as if they were fighting a boardroom battle in which no children or family structure was involved. I understand it's easy to bash attorneys these days, and I understand the many ways in which attorneys provide a useful function, some of which I've benefited from. But some attorneys frequently cross ethical lines to obscure the truth or insert clauses into documents that have no supportable legal basis simply to gain undue advantage for their clients. Unfortunately, outcomes are many times skewed in favor of the party represented by the less ethical attorney.

Also, there is absolutely no legal obligation for an attorney to care whether gaining an advantage for his clients might further damage family dynamics and the separated family's ability to function effectively in the future. Maybe this isn't an attorney's legal obligation, but it should be an ethical and moral consideration.

I don't believe professional counselors are utilized in the divorce process as much as they should be. Cost may be a deterrent in some situations, but I believe attorneys should be required to solicit a family counselor's input to assess if a divorce settlement takes the children's best interests into consideration. Since many divorces don't involve the custody court (for any number of reasons) family counselors are often the only ones trained to make qualified custody suggestions and recommendations.

I also strongly believe that having the involvement of a professional counselor can serve as a check on attorneys who scratch each other's back in ways that enhance their fees but provide little actual value. Counselors would be in a better position to recommend certain attorneys to their clients based on first-hand experience. Also, if counselors are more involved, attorneys who push ethical boundaries too far might find it more difficult to justify their actions.

Regarding attorneys, those who practice family and divorce law should be required to undergo sensitivity training. They are too often in a position to cause outcomes that don't take into account the future functionality of the family they are helping to legally break apart.

Writing this book has helped me realize that I am interested in becoming active in ways that can effect positive changes in all aspects of the divorce process. I'm specifically interested in helping to advocate for efforts to reduce legal abuse by ex-spouses and their representatives, and to enable civil action against ex-spouses who alienate the children from their parent.

Finally, I hope my girls might one day read this account of what really took place and will have a better understanding of how I never wanted to be separated from them. I think about them every day and miss them more than ever. I hope someday we will be able to share the same type of love we enjoyed in so many ways for so long.

Book Recommendation:

"Overcoming the Devastation of Legal Abuse Syndrome" by Karin Huffer, M.S., M.F.T.

Chapter 15

National Coalition Against Parental Alienation

We recently founded National Coalition Against Parental Alienation (NCAPA) in order promote awareness and solutions for PAS. NCAPA is a non-profit 501(c)(3) corporation.

The NCAPA website is located at www.againstPAS.org .

NCAPA has contracted for the exclusive digital/online publishing rights for the book *Parental Alienation: The Handbook for Mental Health and Legal Professionals*, edited by Demosthenes Lorandos, William Bernet, and S. Richard Sauber. We have created online educational and training courses based in significant part on the book….one course is for the family counseling, mental health, and legal professions, and a separate course is for parents and family members.

NCAPA's goal is to be a leading international resource for PAS education, training, awareness, and solutions.

In addition to the training courses, the NCAPA website outlines important PAS tenets and definitions, and includes a petition which members can support which is available for reference by others involved in efforts to implement solutions.

I can be reached at Richard@againstPAS.org

My heart goes out to those who suffer from the alienation of their child(ren).

My appreciation goes out to those who are willing to join the effort to help end the abuses that PAS inflicts on children and parents.

Made in the USA
Lexington, KY
12 June 2018